THE
Product
Manager's
Field Guide

THE
Product Manager's Field Guide

PRACTICAL TOOLS, EXERCISES,
AND RESOURCES FOR IMPROVED
PRODUCT MANAGEMENT

Linda Gorchels

McGraw·Hill

New York   Chicago   San Francisco   Lisbon   London   Madrid   Mexico City
Milan   New Delhi   San Juan   Seoul   Singapore   Sydney   Toronto

Library of Congress Cataloging-in-Publication Data

Gorchels, Linda.
    The product manager's field guide : practical tools, exercises, and resources
for improved product management / Linda Gorchels.
        p.   cm.
    Includes bibliographical references and index.
    ISBN 0-07-141059-7
    1. Product management.   2. New Products—Marketing.   I. Title.

HF5415.15.G635   2003
658.5—dc21   2002044488

1 2 3 4 5 6 7 8 9 0 DOC/DOC 2 1 0 9 8 7 6 5 4 3

ISBN 0-07-141059-7

Interior design by Think Design Group

McGraw-Hill books are available at special quantity discounts to use as premiums and
sales promotions, or for use in corporate training programs. For more information, please
write to the Director of Special Sales, Professional Publishing, McGraw-Hill, Two Penn
Plaza, New York, NY 10121-2298. Or contact your local bookstore.

This book is printed on acid-free paper.

Contents

CHAPTER 5

Financial Foundations of Planning   75

CHAPTER 6

Product and Brand Portfolio Analysis   93

CHAPTER 7

Strategic Visioning and Planning   107

CHAPTER 8

Concept and Development of New Products   121

CHAPTER 9

Launch Guidelines for New Products   143

THE
Product
Manager's
Field Guide

1

Assets of Influential Product Managers

"Hold yourself responsible for a higher standard than anybody else expects of you."

—Henry Ward Beecher,
Nineteenth-century essayist

Product managers typically have job descriptions listing duties and responsibilities, such as competitive analysis and new product development.[1] These itemized lists identify the requirements of the job and are used to measure an employee's success. They provide the *what* of the job, but they don't always include the *how*—the personal characteristics that influence performance. How should product managers develop their capabilities to successfully perform the duties listed in the job description? What are the skills, abilities, knowledge, and traits that comprise the competency set that distinguishes outstanding performers from average performers? Product manager behaviors drive performance, and competencies drive behavior.

Identifying competencies is a process of discovery. Many companies start by analyzing top performers to uncover "secrets" to their success, and/or compile general information from outside sources. This internal analysis is useful for industry-specific competency requirements, whereas the external analysis allows a broader benchmarking perspective. In either situation, the competencies should be truly related to effective performance as a product manager. Perhaps the best

---

1. For more information on the organizational structure of product management and the cross-functional role of product managers, refer to the first three chapters of Linda Gorchels, *The Product Manager's Handbook* (Chicago: NTC Business Books, 2000).

approach is to obtain general competencies from external sources and adapt them to the specific requirements of a company or industry.[2]

Let's start with a general definition of product management:

Product management is the entrepreneurial management of a piece of business (product, product line, service, brand, segment, etc.) as a "virtual" company, with a goal of long-term customer satisfaction and competitive advantage.

- Product managers are generally accountable for this piece of business without having direct authority over the entities (e.g., employees and suppliers) that "make it happen."
- Product management may include, but is not synonymous with, project management, new product development, or sales support.

Keeping this general definition in mind, what are the competencies associated with success? To be able to manage a piece of business, product managers need a solid background in business skills. To be able to attain these results without direct authority over all of the people involved requires an ability to work through other people. To ensure customer satisfaction and competitive advantage, product managers must understand customers and infuse this knowledge throughout the organization. They must also be able to translate this customer information into technologically specific product and service requirements. And finally, since product managers deal with new product development, numerous projects, and ongoing sales support activities, time management, project management, and organizational skills are essential.

Several competencies are associated with top-performing product managers. These competencies can be grouped into five behavioral clusters (as shown in the competency model in Figure 1.1) surrounding the entrepreneurial traits and skills required to do the job. The clusters highlight the necessary abilities to:

1. drive business results
2. deliver results through people
3. ensure market-driven direction
4. guide product "fit" and function
5. manage multiple priorities

---

2. For more information on identifying and using competencies, refer to Jim Kochanski, "Competency-Based Management," *Training & Development*, October 1997, pp. 40–44.

FIGURE 1.1 *Product Manager Competency Model*

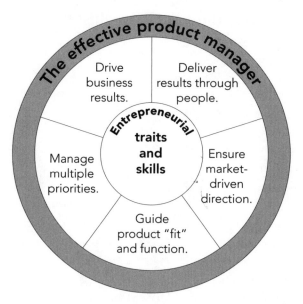

Each of the five clusters contains different competencies that will apply to product managers in varying degrees, depending on the company and industry. It is useful to observe these competencies in top-performing product managers in your firm and augment the general set of requirements here with specifics unique to your situation. This chapter gives an overview of these competencies, which are then presented in more depth in subsequent chapters.

Drive Business Results

The product manager's job is to oversee all aspects of a product or service line to create and deliver superior customer satisfaction while simultaneously providing long-term value for the company. To be able to drive business results for a given area of responsibility, skills in business fundamentals (such as strategy, finance, and planning) are critical. A description of the general skills is provided in the sidebar on pages 4 and 5.

This competency set is perhaps the most concrete since performance can be measured with standard business metrics such as revenue, profit, or return on investment. Weaknesses are also more visible, allowing product managers to

Competency Set One: The Ability to Drive Business Results

STRATEGIC APPRAISAL
- identify capabilities and skills of the business
- identify and appraise commercial opportunities
- prepare background material and interpret external trends
- integrate planning assumptions and premises
- identify key issues, opportunities, and threats
- translate corporate direction and strategic thrust into product portfolio decisions

Do I have a clear vision and strategic plan for my products?

MARKETING AND BUSINESS PLANNING
- translate strategy into action plans
- specify targets and milestones
- ensure plans are consistent with other parts of the company
- develop forecasts for sales and manufacturing
- establish positioning and value proposition
- formulate pricing strategies and tactics
- integrate marketing communications (trade shows, advertising, PR, etc.)
- contribute to sales channel strategies
- establish demand generation programs
- maintain backup plans
- implement plans within established budget

Have I converted my strategy into a plan with measurable objectives in terms of revenue and growth?

focus more clearly on areas of improvement. The remaining competencies are more subjective and require efforts in personal development. Before we move on to the next competency set, take some time to determine how well aligned you are to the targeted competencies that are part of *Driving Business Results*.

Alignment Exercise

Evaluate your experience and knowledge related to each area and determine whether your skill level is (1) deficient, (2) basically competent, (3) proficient, or (4) advanced. These will be the four self-rating categories to use for each of the alignment exercises in this chapter.

FINANCIAL KNOWLEDGE AND SKILLS

- work with finance and accounting to identify key cost and revenue drivers for product area
- monitor key performance measures (e.g., contribution, return on investment, payback)
- obtain financial evaluations of business options
- assess implications of financial analyses and assumptions
- interpret sensitivity analyses and related business risks
- respond to variance reports and analyses
- link operational actions to financial outcomes
- interpret all financial components of product management, including product contribution margins, profit-and-loss statements, budget processes, and return on investment calculations

Do I fully utilize financial metrics in making decisions for my product(s)?

SELLING KNOWLEDGE AND SKILLS

- ability to prequalify customers
- ability to analyze performance of key accounts
- knowledge of the sales process used by your sales force

Is knowledge of the sales process evident in my plans?

(1) *Deficient.* Product manager lacks some of the necessary experience, skills, or abilities related to this competence.

(2) *Basically Competent.* Product manager is able to perform these competencies on a fundamental level and understand the knowledge sufficiently to be able to carry out an in-depth discussion and participate in making decisions.

(3) *Proficient.* Product manager is able to perform these competencies on a fully operational level and understand them well enough to teach others, if necessary.

(4) *Advanced.* Product manager is not only fully proficient in these competencies, but also pushes the competency to a higher level.

Now rate yourself along the attributes of *Driving Business Results*.

Strategic appraisal	1	2	3	4
Marketing and business planning	1	2	3	4
Financial knowledge and skills	1	2	3	4
Selling knowledge and skills	1	2	3	4

Unless you rated yourself "4" for all of these criteria, there may be areas in which you want to improve. You can create a self-improvement plan to advance your competence in the selected area(s). The plan could include books, seminars, classes, membership in related professional organizations, and/or volunteering for committees or boards of civic groups and associations that would allow you to develop the appropriate business skills.

Deliver Results Through People

The business skills mentioned here help drive results, but most product managers must implement their plans through other people—people they have no direct line authority over. This is similar to situations where entrepreneurs need to use their interpersonal skills to be able to borrow money from the bank, outsource manufacturing capabilities, and convince independent representatives and distributors to embrace their products. Product managers face similar entrepreneurial challenges and are consequently general managers of "virtual" companies. It is critical that product managers don't fall prey to the "victim mentality"—a belief that everything is beyond their control and they are therefore powerless. Product managers must be self-confident about their own competence and their ability to lead others.

To deliver results through people, product managers must be able to lead upward, downward, and sideways. Leading up can require perseverance and fortitude. Not all superiors want (or even welcome) recommendations from below. But if a product manager is to participate in propelling a company toward its strategic goals, he or she must supply top management (and possibly boards of directors) with strategic insight, timely advice, and realistic options as they relate to a given product portfolio. Michael Useem, in *Leading Up: How to Lead Your Boss So You Both Win*, provides several useful tips on the topic:

LESSONS IN LEADING UP[3]

- Disdain and contempt for your superior . . . will be returned in kind, thus shortening your leash and limiting your assets.
- Withholding vital information from above is sure to make your superior's job more difficult and damage his or her trust in you.
- A bias for action is what your superior wants.
- Learning to question your boss behind closed doors . . . will get your ideas into the room and keep power struggles out of it.
- If your decisions serve the mission [of the organization], they will ultimately serve your superiors as well.
- Due diligence is everything. Without detailed intelligence on the conditions the organization faces, senior people will be unable to make fast, accurate decisions in response to requests from below.
- Overconfidence in your governing board's confidence in you is sure to blind you to the moves you should be making to ensure you retain its trust.
- Asking your boss to elaborate and clarify inadequate instructions can make the difference between survival and success.

According to Webster's Collegiate Dictionary, *influence* is "the power or capacity of causing an effect in indirect or intangible ways." Effective product managers display an ability to influence others through clear communication, expertise, trust, commitment, and follow-through. There are several points to remember about verbal or oral communication. First, total behavior is involved in oral communication. Words, tone of voice, and body language all contribute to the message being conveyed, with the relative importance of each varying by circumstance. Second, communication requires a sender and a receiver. If the intended receiver has not heard or understood your message, you have not truly communicated. Therefore, ask questions to assure that the listener understood what you intended. Finally, communication improves when you practice empathic listening—putting yourself in the other person's shoes. Anticipate the "hot points" for that type of function, level, or company. For example, the CFO may want to know the likely impact a decision will have on the company stock price, the VP-Operations may wonder if it will require capacity changes, and

---

3. For more detail, refer to Michael Useem, *Leading Up: How to Lead Your Boss So You Both Win* (New York: Crown Business, 2001).

Competency Set Two: Ability to Deliver Results Through People

COMMUNICATION

- communicate effectively with several types and levels of staff and external contacts, both in writing and verbally
- liaison between sales and technical product development team
- write customer-focused requirements in a language appropriate for internal designers
- negotiate and interact with diverse personality types
- listen with open attitude
- prepare and give group presentations on marketing and sales strategy and proposed new product development, including ROI calculations, competitive analysis, customer needs, critical success factors, market analysis, sales justification, and so forth

Do I provide clear oral and written messages to all types and levels of people I deal with?

INFLUENCE AND POLITICS

- adapt style and approach to suit different audiences
- seek to build rapport and gain support and commitment
- act to gain support for ideas before decision-making meetings
- maintain a valuable network of contacts across business areas
- involve others in decisions in order to build ownership for changes
- act to build long-term relationships with customers and stakeholders
- manage complex external relationships for the benefit of the organization

Am I able to convince, inspire, motivate, and encourage others to move toward a significant vision or goal?

other managers may be concerned that it will require more work on their part than it is worth.

To move from communication to influence, product managers must actively shape and enlarge their audiences, and develop a leadership agenda that is a road map for gaining the commitment and support of others. Several questions help frame the road map.

- Who are the critical constituencies or stakeholders in the results?
- Whose cooperation will be necessary to accomplish your goals?

INTERACTING WITH THE SALES FORCE

- build trust and motivation among the sales force
- provide appropriate training to help salespeople sell
- collaborate with sales managers
- build network of "advisors" within sales force
- assist in closing sales, as appropriate
- identify types of sales tools most appropriate for specific types of sales situations

> *Have I proven myself among the sales force sufficiently to gain their trust and commitment?*

DEVELOPING OTHERS (MOST RELEVANT FOR SENIOR PRODUCT MANAGERS)

- express positive expectations of others
- create development opportunities for others
- provide sustained mentoring and coaching to develop skills and competencies and guide behavior
- delegate full authority and responsibility to develop specific skills
- create ongoing activities
- ensure subordinates are actively developing their teams
- drive processes for the development of future leaders

> *Do I provide my direct reports with authority and responsibility and enable skill development?*

- Are these people your allies or adversaries? Do they share your vision? Do they trust you? How will you interact differently with them based on this information?
- What do you expect of others, and what can they expect of you?

A critical constituency for many product managers is the sales force. Salespeople develop relationships with customers and want assurance that product management decisions won't damage those relationships. Decisions to discontinue a product line, change pricing strategies, or launch a new product all have the potential to impact certain accounts. Even decisions that are overwhelmingly positive for the overall company and that significantly move it toward a long-term corporate vision can be perceived negatively by some salespeople or some accounts. Product managers must handle these situations to the best of their ability. This requires building trust (through demonstration of technical competence, honesty, and integrity), gaining commitment (by creating and leveraging a network of sales "allies"), and supporting the plan (by providing salespeople with the appropriate tools and incentives to perform).

Although most product managers have few or no direct reports, some companies have "senior product manager" or "product group manager" positions that do have direct reports. For these types of positions, hiring, training, and performance evaluations may be part of the job description. Therefore, the ability to develop the skills and capabilities of direct reports may become a necessary competence.

Alignment Exercise

Evaluate your experience and knowledge related to each area and determine whether your skill level is (1) deficient, (2) basically competent, (3) proficient, or (4) advanced. If the specific skill is not relevant to your position, circle *not applicable* (NA).

Now rate yourself along the attributes of *Deliver Results Through People.*

Communication	1	2	3	4	NA
Influence and politics	1	2	3	4	NA
Interacting with the sales force	1	2	3	4	NA
Developing others	1	2	3	4	NA

As before, develop a self-improvement plan for any competencies you would like to enhance. There are several possible techniques to include in your plan.

- Increase your education and knowledge through books, seminars, classes, and conferences.
- Improve your communication skills by joining groups such as Toastmasters International.
- Identify key constituents (e.g., industry analysts, salespeople, internal allies, significant channel members, etc.) to align yourself with.

- Since improving this competence involves not only who you are but also how others perceive you, solicit this type of information (either informally through colleague conversations or formally through techniques such as 360° feedback).
- Practice, practice, practice.

Ensure Market-Driven Direction

Understanding customers has been a mantra in corporate America for half a century. Yet many companies become so caught up in internal crises and fire fighting that "market focus" is given only lip service. At this point the product manager must step up and bring in the appropriate market-driven focus. The product manager must not only have an "intimate" understanding of customers, but must also act as the customer advocate in the organization.

To be a customer advocate, product managers need to develop a compelling vision of customers' existing and future needs. This vision has to be beyond one customer and focus on the set of customers that comprise "the market." This can occasionally be a challenge for product managers who have just been hired from the sales force and still think about customers in their territory rather than customers in all territories who may be a target for the product(s). Market research and competitive intelligence help ease this transition.

Although not all product managers will personally conduct market surveys, they nevertheless must be able to manage the process. This could involve selecting market research firms and evaluating proposals or working with an internal research department. Regardless of whether the research is conducted by an internal or external group, product managers should be able to assess whether qualitative or quantitative research is most appropriate and interpret the results obtained. (See Chapter 4 for further discussion on this point.)

Competitive intelligence is an aspect of marketing research that helps a product manager determine whether a specific product not only meets customer needs, but whether it does so better than the competition. To do so requires that a product manager have ongoing data on competitive features and benefits, changes in strategy, and other potential impacts on competitiveness.

Armed with appropriate customer, market, and competitive information, product managers can help ensure market-driven direction through their leadership abilities, primarily their ability to lead cross-functional teams.

Competency Set Three: Ability to Ensure Market-Driven Direction

CUSTOMER CHAMPION

- focus outwardly toward customers and the market
- identify and address the underlying/future needs of customers
- continually look for future possibilities from trends
- are passionate about creating value for customers
- act as a champion for customers (markets) in the company

Am I honestly passionate about creating value for the customers in my target market(s)?

MARKET RESEARCH SKILLS

- design, implement, and interpret research
- identify and utilize market demographics
- maintain relationship with lead users and industry analysts
- select and evaluate research firms or projects

Do I have solid data about the market to use in decision making?

COMPETITIVE INTELLIGENCE

- identify strengths and weaknesses of competitors
- establish network among sales force and analysts to develop ongoing stream of competitive information
- continually work to reinforce competitive advantage

Do I have data to prove that the value my products offer customers is superior to that of the competition?

LEADING CROSS-FUNCTIONAL TEAMS

- gain support and respect of cross-functional teams
- participate in the definition of product road maps
- manage information flow to achieve results
- clarify individual and team roles and responsibilities
- develop a compelling vision that generates enthusiasm and energy

Can I articulate a clear and compelling vision to lead the company in a market-driven direction?

Alignment Exercise

Evaluate your experience and knowledge related to each area and determine whether your skill level is (1) deficient, (2) basically competent, (3) proficient, or (4) advanced. If the specific skill is not relevant to your position, circle *not applicable* (NA).

Now rate yourself along the attributes of *Ensure Market-Driven Direction.*

Customer champion	1	2	3	4	NA
Market research skills	1	2	3	4	NA
Competitive intelligence	1	2	3	4	NA
Leading cross-functional teams	1	2	3	4	NA

As before, determine which competencies to focus on in your self-improvement plan. In addition to taking advantage of formal educational opportunities, other tactics to incorporate may include spending more time out in the field with customers and attending speeches given by employees of competitive firms. It may also be useful to establish customer advisory boards, user groups, and distributor or rep councils to provide market information.

Guide Product "Fit" and Function

Product managers strive to gain an intimate knowledge of customers in order to create competitively superior product and service offerings—and to do it profitably for the company. This requires some level of technical and operational knowledge. Product managers must have sufficient knowledge to act as the bridge between customer needs and technical product specifications.

Product managers take the "voice of the customer" and translate customer priorities into product specifications—what is ideally and minimally acceptable. These specifications provide a precise description of *what* the product has to do, not necessarily *how* the product will be made to provide for those needs. Although most product managers won't be doing the actual product designs, they should know whether a certain type or thickness of material will provide the strength the customer requires, or whether a specific medical test will provide the information the customer is looking for.

The level of proficiency in terms of manufacturing, inventory control, or other internal processes will depend on the needs of a specific company.[4] Some product managers are expected to work with suppliers of raw materials on make-or-buy decisions, some are charged with managing product inventory, and some are charged with technical support. In particular, this knowledge may be useful in establishing product platforms and portfolios. There is no right or wrong approach here unless the structure causes the company to lose sight of the customers and the need to satisfy their requirements better than the competition.

Products must "fit" both internally and externally. Does the mix of products enable a complete solution for the customer, or are complementary products missing? Are the products being designed for the primary target customers, or for the general market?

Alignment Exercise

Evaluate your experience and knowledge related to each area and determine whether your skill level is (1) deficient, (2) basically competent, (3) proficient, or (4) advanced. If the specific skill is not relevant to your position, circle *not applicable* (NA).

Now rate yourself along the attributes of *Guide Product "Fit" and Function.*

Technical understanding	1	2	3	4	NA
Quality control and operations knowledge	1	2	3	4	NA
Product portfolio analysis	1	2	3	4	NA
New product development	1	2	3	4	NA

In addition to various educational opportunities to improve performance within these competencies, it may be useful to participate in some job rotation or job shadowing to learn more about the technical side of the product manager's job.

---

4. If an understanding of manufacturing is important, a concise discussion of product architecture and design for manufacturability can be found in Karl Ulrich and Steven Eppinger, *Product Design and Development* (New York: McGraw-Hill, 1995).

Competency Set Four: Ability to Guide Product "Fit" and Function

TECHNICAL UNDERSTANDING
- knowledge of the technical requirements of the product or service *(This section will be unique to each company or industry. It would include specific knowledge and experience such as back-end server technologies, laboratory assays in molecular biology, or telecom infrastructure services.)*
- ability to translate technical writing into user-friendly customer documentation

Do I have sufficient technical knowledge to be able to act as liaison between customers and staff?

QUALITY CONTROL AND OPERATIONS KNOWLEDGE
- quality control fundamentals
- mastery of basic manufacturing principles
- knowledge of inventory, warehousing, and logistics as appropriate

Can I talk knowledgeably with internal operations staff about product needs?

PRODUCT PORTFOLIO ANALYSIS
- manage product lifecycle from concept to grave
- recommend future products

- develop product launch requirements
- oversee brand asset management
- track product releases
- participate in trademark and logo decisions
- participate in category management issues

Can I articulate how each of my products "fits" within my product portfolio and within the overall company?

NEW PRODUCT DEVELOPMENT
- focal point to ensure all members of product development teams are moving in the same direction
- ability to turn features into benefits, products into solutions
- develop customer-friendly new product ideas
- drive engineering requirements and process development toward the customer
- manage product launch to reach appropriate customers

Do I manage the new product projects to ensure that initial specifications are maintained unless specific market changes dictate otherwise?

Manage Multiple Priorities

The fifth and final behavioral competency set of the competency model is the ability to manage multiple priorities. Product managers must be able to see the big picture while managing details and schedules. No amount of strategy or planning skills training, however, can create competent product managers if they lack the ability to manage their projects and themselves.

Nearly a decade ago the Center for Creative Leadership (CCL) reported that the typical manager or professional:

- Works nearly 10 hours a week longer than a decade earlier.
- Retains 35 hours of backlogged work on his desk.
- Is often stretched too thin to pay more than lip service to improving internal customer service.[5]

Things have not improved for the first decade of the twenty-first century. Product managers, in particular, tend to become overwhelmed with data collection and fire fighting to the detriment of the longer-term aspects of the job, and they frequently procrastinate. They will often pick up and put down the same piece of work many times before acting on it. Another CCL study showed "that the average mid-level manager is interrupted every 5 to 20 minutes."[6] These interruptions have a negative impact on the efficiency of any knowledge worker, including product managers.

Alignment Exercise

Evaluate your experience and knowledge related to each area and determine whether your skill level is (1) deficient, (2) basically competent, (3) proficient, or (4) advanced. If the specific skill is not relevant to your position, circle *not applicable* (NA).

Now rate yourself along the attributes of *Manage Multiple Priorities*.

Time management	1	2	3	4	NA
Project management	1	2	3	4	NA

---

5. Ira Chaleff, "Overload Can Be Overcome," *Industry Week*, June 7, 1993, pp. 44+.

6. Chaleff, *Industry Week*, pp. 44+.

Competency Set Five: Ability to Manage Multiple Priorities

TIME MANAGEMENT

- front-end screen all publications, reports, and data to determine what is important and what can be eliminated
- reduce the number of E-mail, subscription, and report-distribution lists you are on
- prioritize activities based on an awareness of overall business goals
- block out time for planning
- filter out nonessential data (including use of E-mail screens and filters)
- reduce procrastination
- handle daily paperwork only once
- reduce interruptions by "batching" communications
- develop organized storage and filing systems to enable easy retrieval
- have only one project on your desk at a time

Do I manage my time, my paperwork, and my plans efficiently?

PROJECT MANAGEMENT

- develop reasonable schedules
- provide for appropriate allocation of resources
- maintain focus and accountability
- handle multiple complex projects at a high level of detail
- define critical paths and time lines
- complete substantial projects on time and within budget through the application of project management principles and techniques
- define new product development projects
- manage the new product project team
- control projects to deliver successful new products

Do I understand and utilize the principles of project management?

Entrepreneurial Skills and Traits

The central part of the product manager competency model consists of entrepreneurial skills and traits. Product managers who possess these traits are passionate and motivated to succeed. They are self-starters who are comfortable being held accountable for results and enjoy problem solving.

Several traits are commonly associated with entrepreneurs: a high energy level, a "can-do" attitude, risk acceptance, hard work, and persistence. On the other hand, entrepreneurs can sometimes get too close to their product or service and not see the flaws that are evident to customers. Product managers must strive to embody the positive attributes of an entrepreneurial drive while controlling or minimizing the negative aspects.

Creating the Product Manager Scorecard

Each of the previous competencies will not have the same weight for all product managers. The level will depend on several factors.

1. **Position level.** An associate product manager may require a basic skill or understanding of a given competence, whereas a senior product manager may need to be proficient.
2. **Organizational structure.** Some companies will have technical product managers, product marketing managers, upstream and/or downstream product managers, and other variations of the position. These variations will dictate that different weights be placed on the competencies that match the needs of the job.
3. **Industry.** Some industries will require a higher level of technical, consumer, or specialized knowledge that will need to be reflected in the weightings.

Using the weightings appropriate for your firm, a product manager scorecard can be developed that combines position weights with individual ratings to highlight possible areas of improvement. See Figure 1.2 for an example of such a scorecard.

To complete the Product Manager Scorecard, decide on the appropriate level of competence for a given product manager position. Determine whether the ideal product manager should be competent, proficient, or advanced for the given item and put that in the column titled "competency weight." The individual product manager ratings against these criteria can be placed in the final column. Then, comparing the two columns, mark the item(s) that, if improved, would make a real difference in how you do your job.

FIGURE 1.2 *Product Manager Scorecard*

COMPETENCY	COMPETENCY WEIGHT	PRODUCT MANAGER RATING
Drive business results.		
Strategic appraisal		
Marketing and business planning		
Financial knowledge and skills		
Selling knowledge and skills		
Deliver results through people.		
Communication		
Influence and politics		
Interacting with the sales force		
Developing others		
Ensure market-driven direction.		
Customer champion		
Market research skills		
Competitive intelligence		
Leading cross-functional teams		
Guide product "fit" and function.		
Technical understanding		
Quality control and operations knowledge		
Product portfolio analysis		
New product development		
Manage multiple priorities.		
Time management		
Project management		

KEY POINTS

- Perform as an entrepreneurial leader of a "virtual" company.
- Have a clear vision, strategy, and measurable plan for your product (*drive business results*).
- Know how to convince, inspire, motivate, and encourage others to move toward the vision (*deliver results through people*).
- Maintain objective data to guarantee that the value your products offer target customers is superior to that of the competition (*ensure market-driven direction*).
- Relate the technical requirements of your products to market needs and create a solid portfolio of offerings (*guide product "fit" and function*).
- Be competent in time and project management skills (*manage multiple priorities*).

2

Project and Time Management Foundations

"Besides the noble art of getting things done, master the noble art of leaving things undone. The wisdom of life consists in the elimination of nonessentials."

—Lin Yutang, Chinese mystic

There is occasionally confusion between the role descriptions of *product* managers and *project* managers. Both positions cut across functional lines of an organization, both require political sensitivity, both have to be conscious of big picture issues and details simultaneously, and both are frequently transitions from positions of technical expertise. However, product managers have numerous responsibilities beyond project management,[1] and project managers handle numerous projects unrelated to the role of a product manager (everything from implementing a new software system to organizing an office move). The first part of this chapter focuses on the *process* of project management that may be relevant to the job of a product manager.[2]

---

1. For examples of typical responsibilities of product managers, refer to the appendix containing sample product management job descriptions in Linda Gorchels, *The Product Manager's Handbook* (Chicago: NTC Business Books, 2000) pp. 253–268. In addition, Chapter 2 addresses the responsibilities of product managers and others in a firm.

2. A related function is *program* manager, the term used to identify individuals who oversee an entire set of projects.

The term *project management* is generally applied to situations where there are several people involved in accomplishing the objectives of a stated project. When there is just one person involved in a project, some of the concepts of prioritization and scheduling may be appropriate but, more significantly, self-management and time management skills are required. Since product managers are involved in *both* multi-person and single-person projects, this chapter also incorporates time management concepts.

Project Management Fundamentals

A typical definition of a project is "a multitask job that has performance, time, cost, and scope requirements and that is done only one time."[3] Note that the definition contains four interrelated constraints: <u>performance, time, cost, and scope</u>. If one constraint changes, it will have an impact on one or more of the others. For example, if the project needs to be completed faster than initially planned, it will likely cost more and/or have reduced performance characteristics. Note also that the definition indicates that a project is a one-time event. It has a definite beginning and end. Example projects that a product manager might be involved with include new product development, a major advertising campaign, a product recall, opening a new service location, or new product sales training.

Required Skills

Before discussing the steps in project management, let's look at what project managers need to do. A project manager should be able to:

- assess trade-offs
- lobby for adequate resources
- identify and acquire personnel appropriate for the project
- motivate team members
- overcome obstacles

Given that companies have limited financial and human resources, trade-offs will constantly need to be made between and within projects. Project managers

---

3. James P. Lewis, *Fundamentals of Project Management* (New York: AMACOM, 2001) p. 2. The book provides a concise overview of the foundation and terminology of project management.

must be aware of the relative priorities of projects as they relate to the mission and vision of the overall company. They must also prioritize various activities and tasks, or sacrifice one or more of the constraints mentioned earlier, and/or lobby for more resources in order to accomplish the original goals.

A critical resource for a project is the right people to do the job. Specific sales-people, engineers, or administrators might personify the qualities most necessary for a given project, but they may need to be "borrowed" from related depart-ments. The project manager must negotiate with the various functional depart-ment managers, and sometimes with the individuals themselves, to attain the appropriate staff for the task. Once on the project team, the individuals will need continual motivation, and the project manager will have to facilitate cooperation among potentially disparate team members. This will require a shared vision, input from the team on the project plan, constant communication, and excellent interpersonal skills.

Even with careful project planning and selection of team members, obstacles will still arise. Last-minute schedule changes, resource conflicts, or changing cus-tomer expectations can pose significant impediments. Project managers need to be flexible, practice open communication, and maintain a solid relationship with a champion high in the organization.

Alignment Exercise

Evaluate your experience and knowledge related to each area and determine whether your skill level is (1) deficient, (2) basically competent, (3) proficient, or (4) advanced. These will be the four self-rating categories to use for each of the alignment exercises in this chapter.

(1) *Deficient.* Product manager lacks some of the necessary experience, skills, or abilities related to this competence.

(2) *Basically Competent.* Product manager is able to perform these competencies on a fundamental level and understand the knowledge sufficiently to be able to carry out an in-depth discussion and participate in making decisions.

(3) *Proficient.* Product manager is able to perform these competencies on a fully operational level and understand them well enough to teach others, if necessary.

(4) *Advanced.* Product manager is not only fully proficient in these competencies, but also pushes the competency to a higher level.

Now rate yourself along the required skills of a project manager, as to whether you have the ability to:

Assess trade-offs	1	2	3	4
Lobby for adequate resources	1	2	3	4
Identify and acquire appropriate personnel	1	2	3	4
Motivate team members	1	2	3	4
Overcome obstacles	1	2	3	4

Unless you rated yourself "4" for all of these criteria, there may be areas in which you want to improve. You can create a self-improvement plan to advance your competence in the selected area(s). The plan could include books, seminars, and classes that would allow you to develop the appropriate skills.

A project manager should also be familiar with the general steps in project management: problem definition, planning and scheduling, managing the team, and controlling and auditing the process.

Problem Definition

Although the problem to be solved may appear clear-cut to the product manager, it must also be clear to everyone on the project team. Therefore, several questions should be answered, as listed here.

- Who is the customer or client for the project?
- What outcomes does the customer desire?
- What is the deadline for completion of the project?
- What is the budget (or proposed cost) for the project?
- What are the relative priorities of the outcomes, deadline, and budget?
- Why did the problem appear at this time?

The problem definition should state where you are now and where you want to go. What is the gap between where you are and where you would like to be? The plan attempts to explain how to close the gap, but it can only do so by recognizing the obstacles that exist. Be sure that the customer is never forgotten during problem definition—and that the project will truly satisfy the customer's needs rather than what the project team *thinks* will satisfy the customer's needs.

Planning and Scheduling the Project

This phase converts the problem definition into solution steps. It provides the map that will be used not only for project execution but also to provide a means of managing and controlling progress. The project plan will contain a problem statement (i.e., a summary of the previous phase), project objectives, schedules, required resources, and a defined control system.

The *project objectives* list the desired outcomes or end results to be achieved. They specify *what* will be achieved, but not *how*. Objectives should be specific and measurable and contain a time frame or deadline. For example, objectives for a product recall might include statements such as:

- to inform all warrantee customers of the recall by August 1, 2004
- to contact all relevant industry media about the recall by August 14, 2004
- to attain a 45 percent recall rate by December 30, 2004

The starting point for *scheduling* the project is identification of the major activities required to complete the project. Each of these activities, in turn, is further broken down into specific tasks and subtasks, creating what is referred to as a *work breakdown structure* or WBS. This information is then used to estimate the time and resource requirements of the project. Therefore, the work tasks must be broken down to a level sufficient to allow acceptable estimates. Without the WBS, any estimates of time and resources will be nothing more than ballpark figures that may be substantially different from actual requirements. Following is a partial example of a WBS for a product recall:

Example Work Breakdown Structure: Product Recall
1000 Conduct comprehensive safety analysis
    1001 Classify risks according to industry/government standards
    1002 Plant visits
    1003 Employee interviews
    1004 Product and equipment tests
    1005 Determine speed of recall

2000 Inform employees
    2001 E-mail all employees
    2002 Establish link on intranet
    2003 Workshop for salespeople on handling the recall in the field

3000 Inform intermediaries and customers
    3001 First-class or priority mailing
    3002 Phone contact with key accounts
    3003 Toll-free hotline for answering questions
    3004 FAQ section on website
    3005 Press releases to relevant media

4000 Recover the recalled product
    4001 Channel inventory program
    4002 Channel assistance for customer returns
    4003 Direct customer returns

5000 Ensure repair or replacement in a timely manner
    5001 Internal procedures
    5002 External procedures

Once the particular activities and tasks are identified, capture their sequential and parallel relationships. What activities can be done simultaneously, and which ones can only happen in a specific order? This is frequently shown as a flowchart, such as Figure 2.1. In this example, Activities A and B can be completed at the same time as C and D, although A precedes B and C precedes D, and all must precede E.

The estimated times for each activity indicate that C-D-E takes the most time and is therefore the *critical path*—the sequence of activities that has no slack and that will delay the entire project if not kept on schedule. The process of constructing a network diagram such as this is called the *Critical Path Method* (CPM). When probabilities are added to the estimated times, the process is called *Program Evaluation and Review Technique* (PERT). Note that even though the activities in Figure 2.1 were drawn in boxes (referred to as an activity-on-node network), the network could also be drawn with the activities on arrows connected by circles representing the completion of the activities (referred to as an activity-on-arrow network).

Managing the Project Team

Simply constructing a CPM or PERT network is not the challenging part of project management—determining what inputs to put into the process is the challenge. It's critical that the various individuals or functional areas that will be

FIGURE 2.1 *CPM Chart*

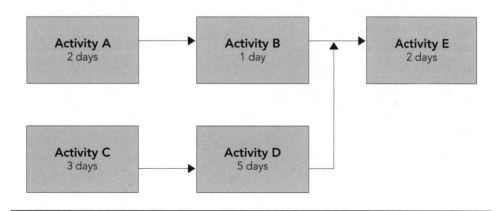

involved in the execution of the project provide input into the time and *resource requirements* of the various activities. The initial network developed from the preliminary inputs will define the expected budget and end point. If either of these is unacceptable, it's necessary to revisit the objectives, shift resources from noncritical to critical path activities, and/or substitute lower cost alternatives into the process. Once an acceptable project schedule has been developed, however, future changes should be minimized as much as possible.

Controlling and Auditing the Project

The project plan and schedule put in place prior to the execution of the project serve as tools of a *control system*. In this case, control refers to comparing the progress against the plan so that corrective action can be taken when deviations occur. Bar charts (also known as Gantt charts) are commonly used to visualize expected versus actual progress along the activities, as shown in Figure 2.2. Note that Activity B is ahead of schedule (since it was scheduled to be completed by Day 3 and has been completed by Day 2—today's date). Activity C is behind schedule by a full day. Since C is part of the critical path, the project is getting behind schedule and corrective action should be taken.

Keep in mind that this plan is a *macro* plan of the total project. Since the project activities are performed by many individuals, most of whom do not report to you, the project manager, there should also be *micro* plans for the individual activities that the team members can control themselves. In addition, there should be critical points in the project at which progress is assessed.

FIGURE 2.2 *Gantt Chart*

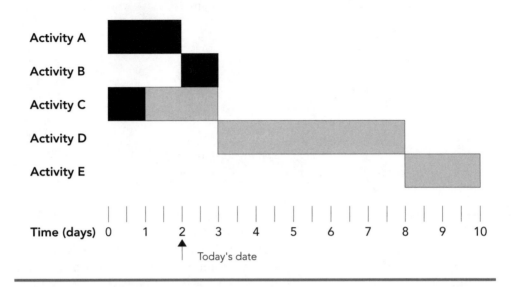

Alignment Exercise

Select a recently completed project to use for self-evaluation. Evaluate your experience and knowledge related to each area and determine whether your skill level is (1) deficient, (2) basically competent, (3) proficient, or (4) advanced. If the specific skill is not relevant to your position, circle *not applicable* (NA).

Now rate yourself on the steps of project management.

Problem definition	1	2	3	4	NA
Planning and scheduling the project	1	2	3	4	NA
Managing the project team	1	2	3	4	NA
Controlling and auditing the project	1	2	3	4	NA

Time Management

For ongoing activities and tasks, as well as for projects in which the activities and tasks are primarily the responsibility of the product manager, effective time management is critical. I will focus here on two primary aspects of time management: efficiency and effectiveness. *Efficiency* is defined as the degree of productivity without waste. *Effectiveness* is defined as the quality of prioritizing and working on the right things. Both aspects implicitly recognize the value of time (see Figure 2.3) but in subtly different ways.

Efficiency

Efficiency in time management requires organization, discipline, and project scheduling efforts. Organizational skills are necessary to minimize time spent looking for things. How much time do you spend searching for files and information that should be at your fingertips? Do you have a filing system that allows you to access the right information quickly? Here are some quick organizational tips:[4]

- Keep current files on top of your desk or in the front of the cabinet.
- Create a logical filing system for other items (including business cards and industry articles).
- Maintain a to-do list system that works for you.
- Throw unnecessary things away!

The best systems in the world will not work unless you have the discipline to make them work. Some time management principles are a matter of will. If you are disciplined in time management, you will do the following:

- Avoid procrastination with a "do it now" attitude.
- Take a "read file" along with you when traveling.
- Create (and follow) meeting agendas, confirm attendance prior to the meeting, and incorporate action steps in the minutes.
- Start and end meetings on time.
- Schedule your own time so that important tasks are done when you operate at your personal best, and so that you can avoid interruptions.
- Practice the art of saying no to unimportant activities.

A major category of discipline is the scheduling of individual projects. Many product managers operate in perpetual fire-fighting mode because they devote more time to putting out fires than to preventing them. Just as individuals break down the multifunctional team projects into their component parts, so must

---

4. For some fast ideas on improving your time management, refer to David Cottrell and Mark C. Layton, *175 Ways to Get More Done in Less Time* (Dallas: CornerStone Leadership Institute, 2000).

FIGURE 2.3 *The Value of Time*

Imagine there is a bank that credits your account each morning with $86,400. It carries over no balance from day to day. Every evening it deletes whatever part of the balance you failed to use during the day.

What would you do? Draw out every cent, of course! Each of us has such a bank. It's name is TIME. Every morning, it credits you with 86,400 seconds. Every night it writes off, as lost, whatever of this you have failed to invest to good purpose.

It carries over no balance. It allows no overdraft. Each day it opens a new account for you. Each night it burns the remains of the day. If you fail to use the day's deposit, the loss is yours. There is no going back. There is no drawing against the "tomorrow."

You must live in the present on today's deposit. Invest it so as to get from it the utmost in health, happiness, and success!

The clock is running.
Make the most of today.

To realize the value of ONE YEAR, ask a student who failed a grade.

To realize the value of ONE MONTH, ask a mother who gave birth to a premature baby.

To realize the value of ONE WEEK, ask the editor of a weekly newspaper.

To realize the value of ONE DAY, ask a daily wage laborer with kids to feed.

To realize the value of ONE HOUR, ask the lovers who are waiting to meet.

To realize the value of ONE MINUTE, ask a person who missed the train.

To realize the value of ONE SECOND, ask a person who just avoided an accident.

To realize the value of ONE MILLISECOND, ask the person who won a silver medal in the Olympics.

Treasure every moment that you have! And treasure it more because you shared it with someone special, special enough to spend your time.

And remember that time waits for no one.
Yesterday is history.
Tomorrow a mystery.
Today is a gift.
That's why it's called the present!

Author unknown

Source: www.starteasy.com/ggalore/time

one-person projects be broken down. Let's say that a major report or presentation is due by a certain future date. If the date is far enough into the future, there may be a lack of urgency to begin working on it. Therefore, it's beneficial to break the project down into component parts (a process I call *chunking*) and schedule the completion of each part. To complete the report it may be necessary to contact industry analysts, gather customer information, develop a first draft, revise, and finalize. Work back from the date the report is due and assign a deadline for each of the individual chunks. Then once the deadlines are determined, schedule your own time (e.g., on your calendar) to work on the chunk and treat that deadline as being as real as any other deadline.

Effectiveness

Efficiency in time management may help you accomplish more tasks in less time. But you still need to ascertain whether the tasks matter. That's where effectiveness comes in. When faced with a time crunch, ask yourself, "what is the best use of my time right now?" To answer this question and determine what is *important* (in addition to what is *urgent*), you will need to determine your values and priorities. Personal values and priorities may be different from organizational values and priorities, but the two cannot be totally divorced from each other.

Stephen Covey's book, *First Things First*,[5] espouses a system of prioritizing activities by categorizing them according to their importance and urgency and then assigning them to quadrants using these two parameters, as shown in Figure 2.4. Items that are both urgent and important (Quadrant A) have the potential to become crises and should be handled immediately. Items in Quadrant B, since they are important but not urgent, have the potential to become crises due to procrastination. These are the items that need to be planned and prioritized carefully. Items in Quadrant C are urgent but not important. According to Covey, we spend time on these activities thinking they are part of A. "The noise of urgency creates the illusion of importance. But the actual activities, if they're important at all, are only important to someone else."[6] Activities in Quadrant D are the true time wasters and should be avoided to allow time for activities in the remaining quadrants.

---

5. Stephen R. Covey's *First Things First* (New York: Simon & Schuster, 1994) provides a review of time management literature in the appendix as well as covering the topic throughout the book.

6. Covey, *First Things First*, p. 38.

FIGURE 2.4 *Activity Prioritization for Time Management*

	Urgent	Not Urgent
Important	**A** Handle immediately.	**B** Organize activities related to your vision and values.
Not Important	**C** Avoid treating all urgent activities as important—selectively evaluate.	**D** Minimize or eliminate.

Adapted from Stephen R. Covey, *First Things First* (New York: Simon & Schuster, 1994) p. 37.

Product management, by its very nature, is a function filled with endless requests for information, sales support, and follow-up activities, in addition to the need for strategic product planning. Product managers must consequently be vigilant in using their time effectively. Activities that are related to the brand equity and/or financial performance of your product are important and likely urgent activities. Determine whether these can be chunked and put into your calendar (as mentioned earlier), and whether some steps can be delegated. Don't allow important activities to be put off without building time for them in your calendar.

Alignment Exercise

Evaluate your experience and knowledge related to time management and determine whether your skill level is (1) deficient, (2) basically competent, (3) proficient, or (4) advanced.

Efficiency	1	2	3	4
Effectiveness	1	2	3	4

KEY POINTS

- Assess trade-offs.
- Lobby for adequate resources.
- Identify and acquire appropriate personnel.
- Motivate team members.
- Overcome obstacles.
- Develop the discipline to organize and schedule your time efficiently.
- Continually ask yourself, "what is the best use of my time right now?"

3 Planning Framework

"If a problem has no solution, it may not be a problem, but a fact—not to be solved, but to be coped with over time."

—Shimon Peres, Israeli statesman

There are several types of plans a product manager might be involved with: strategic plans, new product development plans, and annual marketing plans. The plan could be for the corporation, for a division, or for a specific product line. Each of these plans will require a different analytical scope in terms of what information to compile and what subsequent decisions to make. If the scope is not clear, the plan will fall apart. Therefore, *clarifying the scope* is an important predecessor to the planning process.

Clarify Your Scope

- *What is the scale of your plan?* Is it for a product, a product line, a business unit, or a project? Will it address an entire industry or a regional market?
- *Who is the audience?* Will the plan be presented to your boss to incorporate into a larger plan? Is it for a cross-functional team to use for decision making? Will it be built into a strategic plan?
- *When will the plan be implemented?* Is this for next fiscal year? Is it for two to five years into the future?
- *How will the plan fit into a budget or financial requirement?*

There is no one right way to plan. Companies and individuals have adapted various formats to meet their preferences—to do what feels right for their circumstances. However, there are some elements common to most business, product, or marketing plans.

First, all planning processes incorporate a data collection phase. This might be called a situation analysis, background review, environmental scan, or a host of other terms. Whatever it's called, it's the step where the product manager answers the question *where are you now?* This is the factual portion of the planning process.

Next, all successful plans include goals and statements addressing the question *where do you want to go?* Ideally, there should be a long-term goal or vision, as well as one or more annual objectives specifying what you want to accomplish this year to enable you to progress toward the long-term goal.

Third, since there will be a gap between where you are now and where you want to go, that gap should be the focus of the action plan. This part of the plan provides the strategies and tactics to describe how you will accomplish your objectives—how you will move from where you are now to where you want to be. The strategies list the general approach, whereas the tactics are the more detailed activities that comprise the plan.

Finally, the resources (financial and nonfinancial) required to execute the strategies must be determined, and the results of the plan must be tracked. The process is summarized in the planning model in Figure 3.1. The remainder of this chapter will examine each of the elements shown in this model.

Environmental Scan

Once the scope is clear, it's time to start the planning process with the environmental scan in order to answer the question *where are you now?* This is the fact-finding or data collection phase to propel solid decision making later on. There may be several dimensions of an environmental scan including: (a) upstream business goals, (b) your customers and markets, (c) the competitive situation, (d) the business environment for your industry; and (e) an internal assessment.

Upstream Business Goals

Most plans must link with higher-level plans. A departmental goal may be set by a division, and a divisional goal may be set by corporate headquarters or perhaps a holding company. The same is true for many product management plans. What sales volume or profit does the company require from your product line? What

FIGURE 3.1 *Planning Model*

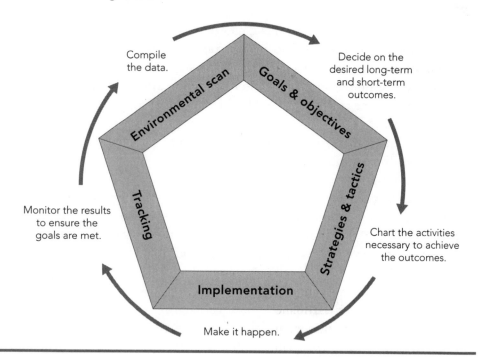

types of new products or services are expected? Are there any growth goals by region or product? Sometimes these expectations are specific enough to become the goals for your plan. In other situations, they are more directional, requiring the product manager to establish the precise quantitative goal statements.

Your Customers and Markets

The single most important part of the environmental scan, and the one most consistent with the product management competency of ensuring market-driven direction, is the analysis of customers and markets. By knowing your best customers in terms of future equity growth, you can profile the target market(s) that become the focal point for your planning efforts. There are several questions to ask about customers:

- Who are your loyal customers? Who are your switchers? Why?
- Who are the users, initiators, influencers, deciders, and purchasers?
- Is your primary target market growing, stable, or declining?

- What trends will change customer needs or behaviors?
- What business(es) are your customers in?
- Who are the customer's customers, and what do they expect?
- What keeps your customers up at night (as it relates to your offerings)?
- What motivates customer-buying decisions?
- What level of support does the customer require after the sale?
- How much of the customer's total business do you have compared to your competitors?
- How difficult is it for your customer to switch to a competitor?
- How does the customer perceive you?

Take a look at the overall market (both customers and noncustomers). What is the size and projected growth rate of the market? What is the size and projected growth rate of different segments within the market? Which appear to offer the greatest profit potential for your specific products? Why?

The Competitive Situation

The next part of the environmental scan is the competitive assessment. For most product management plans, the focus of this part of the environmental scan will be on the comparative strength of competitive advantage between competing offerings and your own offerings. How does your total offering (i.e., product, supporting services, and customer perception) compare with the competition? What data do you (or should you) collect to help you protect or defend your edge against the competition? Some questions to ask about the competition are:

- Who are your competitors today?
- Who might be tomorrow's competitors?
- What business are your competitors in?
- What are their capabilities? Strategies? Goals?
- How can you position yourself in a way that's different?
- What have your competitors done recently to change the competitive arena?
- In the same time period, what have you done to change the competitive arena?
- What can you do to make it more difficult for new and existing competitors to compete against you?
- How might competitors attack you in the future?

The Business Environment for Your Industry

The business environment can include anything external that will have an actual or potential impact on your plan. The business environment could include the price of oil and how it fluctuates, or it could be housing starts, or the availability of food technologists or systems analysts. Some questions to ask about the business environment are:

- What technological changes are likely? How might they impact product sales within the next several years?
- Are there mergers, acquisitions, or divestures among customers, competitors, or channel members that could either derail or assist your plans?
- What leading indictors correspond with product sales? Are they increasing or decreasing?
- What are the national, regional, or local economic trends?
- Are there regulatory or political forces that could impact product sales?
- What is the probability of these trends occurring, and what is their potential financial impact?

Internal Assessment

The internal assessment is an honest appraisal of the strengths and weaknesses surrounding your product. Some questions to ask during your internal assessment are:

- What are the strengths surrounding the product offering from the customer perspective?
- What are the weaknesses surrounding the product offering from the customer perspective?
- Why do these strengths and weaknesses exist?
- How do salespeople and channel members evaluate the product?
- What are the current levels of sales and profitability by product item, by product line, by account, and/or by market segment? Are they acceptable?
- Are price levels competitive?
- How well are your present strategies working?

Step One: Compile Data for an Environmental Scan

- *Are your goals determined or affected by higher-level corporate, division, or business unit goals?* Have they been incorporated into your planning?

- *Do you know who your high-equity customers are?* How are they changing? What do they want in terms of what they buy (features, services, and solutions), where they buy (different channels), when they buy (24/7), how they buy (financing options), and why they buy (purchase drivers)?
- *What do competitors offer that you don't and vice versa?* How has the competitive environment changed?
- *What external trends might affect your product offering?* What is the probability and potential impact of these trends?
- *What are your internal strengths and weaknesses?* How has this changed over time?

Goals and Objectives

After compiling the data as part of the environmental scan, next decide on the desired long-term and short-term outcomes to answer the question *where do you want to go?* The term *goal* generally refers to the fundamental long-term direction, whereas *objectives* break down the broader goal into smaller parts—although the terms are often used interchangeably. A long-term goal could be the strategic vision for a product or a company, and an objective could be how your product will contribute to the goal this year. In either case, they should be precise enough to provide direction for the plan as well as provide a means of evaluating results at the end. In other words, the objectives should be SMART, that is, they should embody several attributes, which are:

Specific
Measurable
Achievable
Results-oriented
Time-based

Let's say you have a goal to "sell as many products as you can." While this may be a worthy goal, how do you know when you have completed it? How can you measure performance? *Specific* objectives are concrete (not wishy-washy), addressing who, what, when, and/or where questions whenever possible. (For example, you may have an objective for your product line to increase the sales of bundled products to select markets.) *Measurable* objectives are numeric or descriptive and may be expressed in terms of sales units, revenue, or growth rates. (By *how much* do you want to increase the sales of the bundled products?) *Achievable* objectives are realistic, and their attainment is within the scope and responsibility of the product manager. (Given information attained during the environmental scan, does it appear reasonable that customers will buy the bundled product?) *Results-oriented* objectives focus on accomplishments or outputs, rather than activities. (Is the focus on the sales of the bundle rather than on the process or activity of putting the bundle together?) *Time-based* objectives identify a target date for reaching the specified results. (By what date will you attain the specified increase in the sales of the bundled products?)

Product managers may be responsible for both strategic product plans and annual marketing plans for their product line. SMART objectives must take into account the specific type of plan. The table in Figure 3.2 highlights the thought process for establishing objectives for an annual marketing plan while nevertheless ensuring a fit with the overall strategic directions of the product or company.

Step Two: Develop Objectives

- *Have you developed SMART objectives?* Are they specific, measurable, achievable, results-oriented, and time-based?
- *Do the objectives provide direction for your plan?*
- *At the end of the planning cycle (e.g., the fiscal year) will you be able to use the objectives as a means of measuring accomplishments?*

Strategies and Tactics

Whereas the objectives indicate *what* is to happen, the strategies and tactics detail *how*. The environmental scan determined *where you are now*, the objectives specified *where you want to go*, and the strategies and tactics of the plan detail *how you are going to get there*. A strategy is the general approach used to achieve the outcomes listed in the objectives; it provides a frame of reference for the subsequent plan, an implicit understanding of why something is being done. The tactics list the more detailed activities that make the strategies happen, that constitute the plan. Many companies blur the distinction between the two terms.

FIGURE 3.2 *Preparing Objectives for a Marketing Plan*

VISION
1. What is the desired future position of the company or product line?

PROBLEMS AND OPPORTUNITIES
1. Draw conclusions from each part of the environmental scan and relate them to the vision.
2. Detail the problems and opportunities to be addressed in the marketing plan.

SALES FORECASTS/GOALS
1. Determine what sales volume is reasonable given historical data and trends in your target market.
2. Obtain sales input from the sales force or distribution channel.
3. Identify what sales are necessary given the financial realities of your business.
4. Reconcile the forecasts.

MARKETING OBJECTIVES AND POSITIONING GOALS
1. Define your primary and secondary target markets/accounts.
2. Determine how much business you have to get from each to attain your sales goal.
3. Write the objectives in terms of the units, dollars, or market share you have to attain from each market within a stated time period.
4. Establish how you want your target customers to perceive your product/service or company relative to the competition (i.e., the positioning goal).

Therefore, they will both be used here to describe the action plan that accomplishes the objectives and goals by capitalizing on opportunities and overcoming problems as identified in the environmental scan.

Let's work through an example. Assume that in conducting the environmental scan you discover that your customers purchase single products rather than the entire product line, resulting in lost opportunities. A possible objective related to this fact could be: "Sell one additional product to 75 percent of existing customers." Strategies and tactics relevant to attaining this objective might include:

- establish quota and incentive programs for sales force to sell appropriate product mix

- educate sales and channel members on the financial impact of selling a full line
- position the company as a provider of one-stop shopping
- bundle products together as a system

Developing strategies and tactics requires some creativity on the part of the product manager. It's always tempting to look for success formulas that can be applied to your products and services without risk. Sometimes these formulas come from other companies and leaders; sometimes they come from past history within the firm. But it's important to remember that strategies have to change as the environment changes. To differentiate yourself in the minds of customers, you have to provide more than the competition. But as you provide more, customers then expect more, competition advances to challenge your unique position, and new areas of differentiation have to be discovered.

The dictionary definition of a strategy is a "cleverly contrived scheme for outwitting the enemy and gaining an end." From a business perspective, a strategy is a plan for outdoing the competition in an effort to win customers and accomplish stated objectives. Theodore Levitt has eloquently stated what he believes to be the requisites of competitive success.

1. The purpose of a business is to create and keep a customer.
2. To do that you have to produce and deliver goods and services that people want and value at prices and under conditions that are reasonably attractive relative to those offered by others to a proportion of customers large enough to make those prices and conditions possible.[1]

As mentioned previously, product managers are commonly responsible for developing annual marketing plans for their products and services.[2] Figure 3.3 lists some of the questions and thought processes that go into preparing appropriate strategies and tactics.

Following Figure 3.3 (on page 45) are some potential strategies and tactics as they relate to example objectives.

---

1. Theodore Levitt, *The Marketing Imagination* (New York: The Free Press, 1986) pp. 5–6.

2. An example outline for writing an annual marketing plan can be found in Figure 7.2, Linda Gorchels, *The Product Manager's Handbook* (Chicago: NTC Business Books, 2000) pp. 113–116.

FIGURE 3.3 *Preparing Strategies and Tactics for an Annual Marketing Plan*

SUMMARY

1. Summarize the key points from the environmental scan to provide support for the core of the marketing plan: the action program.
2. State what aspects of the marketing plan will *not* change from the prior year (e.g., you might not be introducing or modifying products). This will allow you to concentrate on only those marketing tactics you will be changing the next fiscal year to accomplish the stated objectives.

TARGET MARKET(S)

1. Profile the primary and secondary markets to which you will be allocating resources in the remainder of the marketing plan.
2. Identify general differences in marketing to each group. Develop marketing objectives for each target market. If the differences are dramatic, you may need different marketing plans by target.

PRODUCT STRATEGY

1. Explain planned changes in the product, brand identity, and/or packaging.
2. Identify new accessories or any other items.

PRICING STRATEGY

1. Describe planned changes in pricing policies, price points, or list prices.
2. Demonstrate impact on selling and profit performance.

PROMOTION STRATEGY

1. List and describe end customer and channel promotion programs to be used.
2. Describe any changes in cooperative advertising.
3. Define the theme, promise, support, and tone for the advertising message.
4. Identify the appropriate media mix.
5. Develop a media plan with calendar and budget.
6. Mention any significant trade show, merchandising, or publicity programs.

SALES/DISTRIBUTION STRATEGY

1. Mention any structural changes in field sales strategy.
2. Describe programs to improve dealer/distributor/retailer effectiveness.

PRODUCT SUPPORT

1. Define changes in warranty/guarantee policies and programs.
2. List planned changes in customer service or delivery strategies.

OBJECTIVE: Convert 150 Company X Customers to Our Products.
Related strategies/tactics:
- reduce switching costs for competitor's customers
- focus on product exciters
- enable low-risk trial through free samples or limited-time free usage
- honor trade-in of competitive product toward purchase of your products

OBJECTIVE: Increase the Percentage of Products Sold at List Price from X% to Y%.
Related strategies/tactics:
- segment the market based on price sensitivity and target those customers less price sensitive
- establish quota and incentive programs for the sales force based on price realization
- increase product knowledge of staff and salespeople
- develop exclusive channels to protect premium price/brand equity
- create marketing communications that will prove the lifetime value of the purchase
- reposition the product or select features as "classic" or "nostalgic"
- identify new markets or new applications for the product

Step Three: Craft Strategies and Tactics

- *Have you creatively brainstormed ways to accomplish the end results specified in your objectives?* Remember to seek ideas that are different from the competition. Truly creative plans are often contrary to conventional wisdom.
- *Do the strategies and tactics make sense given your environmental scan?* The environmental scan provides the rationale or justification for your plan. Even though creativity is necessary, it has to be balanced with reality.

Implementation

Accountability and communication are the implementation aspects of the planning process. Strategies should be linked with action plans and ways of measuring whether the plans were accomplished. Some measures are straightforward, such as when an objective is to increase sales. However, if a goal is to increase awareness or change customer perceptions, it can be measured directly only through a survey (or indirectly through a change in sales).

People and resources are necessary to implement plans. If either is underestimated, a plan may not accomplish what was intended. Therefore, plans should include a financial budget (perhaps in the form of an income or profit-and-loss statement), and an implementation schedule. An implementation plan can be a simple schedule of names, assignments, and dates. Examples of both follow in Figures 3.4 and 3.5.

The implementation schedule may be appropriate for internal staff and issues, but it will not work for the aspect of implementation that is handled by the sales force. That will require interpersonal skill and persuasion, as discussed in Chapters 1 and 9.

For annual plans, a particular implementation challenge of product managers is to help sales management convert a marketing plan into a sales plan. This requires that market descriptions be converted to account profiles, general sales goals to territory-specific goals, anticipated customer applications to questions the salespeople can ask to determine "fit," and marketing communications to sales communications.

Step Four: Implement the Plan

- *Have you identified—and attained commitment for—the resources (both human and financial) required for the plan?* To prevent your plan from simply sitting on the shelf you will need to aggressively make it happen.
- *Have you communicated your vision and obtained buy-in from others necessary to implement the plan?* True buy-in requires that people not only agree with your vision and strategies, but also are willing to help you put them into action.

Tracking

An outgrowth of implementation is *tracking*. Tracking implies that measures and milestones have been specified to help evaluate progress toward the objectives of the plan. The measures to track should be part of the plan—and require acceptance

FIGURE 3.4 *Product Line X Profit-and-Loss Statement, 20___ Budget*

	PREVIOUS YEAR	PERCENT SALES	CURRENT YEAR	PERCENT SALES	NEXT YEAR	PERCENT SALES
Sales Revenue	$	%	$	%	$	%
Less price adjustment						
Cost of goods						
Gross Margin						
Controllable Marketing Expenses						
Advertising						
Trade allowances						
Promotions						
Trade shows						
Sales support						
Training						
Total Controllable Marketing Expenses						
Other Expenses						
Sales force						
Distribution						
Administration						
Miscellaneous						
Total Other Expenses						
Total Expenses						
Profit Contribution						
Increase/Decrease						

FIGURE 3.5 *Implementation Schedule*

WHAT	WHO	WHEN	HOW MUCH	MEASURES
Activities	Person responsible	Dates, timing	Budget resources	Milestones
1. _____	_____	_____	_____	_____
2. _____	_____	_____	_____	_____
3. _____	_____	_____	_____	_____
4. _____	_____	_____	_____	_____

by the parties who are responsible for plan implementation. Example milestones for a product launch are listed in Chapter 9. Other milestones relate specifically to the stated objectives of a plan. If an objective is to sell X dollars through a new distribution channel by year-end, how much inventory do you want the parties to have in stock by the first quarter? If the objective is to change customer perceptions, a series of small-scale surveys may be desired; are they in progress? Note the linkage between action plans and measures in Figure 3.6.

Step Five: Tracking Plan Execution

- *Have you determined what measures to track and at what specific points in time?* Tracking the progress of the plan helps you identify problems as early as possible, thereby allowing you to take corrective action before it is too late.
- *Do the measures link back to the objectives?* Be careful that you don't track measures that are actually unrelated to the objectives and tactics of the plan.

FIGURE 3.6 *Linking Strategies to Measures*

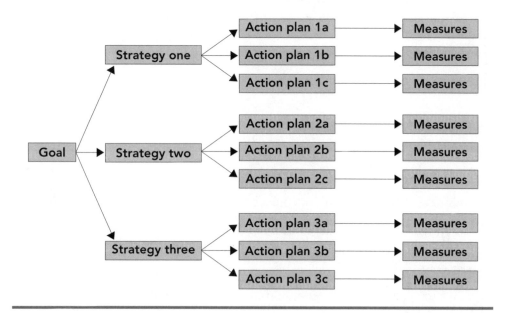

KEY POINTS

- Clarify the scope of your planning (in terms of time, scale, and specific products) as the starting point for your efforts.
- Collect data as part of an environmental scan to provide factual answers to the question, *where are you now?*
- Develop strategies and tactics that close the gap between where you are now and where you want to go.
- Identify and gain commitment from or for the resources necessary to implement the plan.
- Determine specific measures and milestones to track progress toward the attainment of the ultimate objectives and goals.
- Remember, the future is not a place you are going to; it's a place you are creating. And your business plan is a map to take you there.

PLANNING CHECKLIST

CLARIFY SCOPE

Have you defined the scale of your plan?   Yes   No

Is the intended audience for the plan clear?   Yes   No

ENVIRONMENTAL SCAN

Have you listed upstream business goals?   Yes   No

Did you provide a detailed profile of the target customers?   Yes   No

Do you have sufficient detail on competition to justify or
prove your advantage?   Yes   No

Have you explored external trends or events that may
impact your plan?   Yes   No

Have you completed an honest appraisal of your firm's strengths
and weaknesses as they relate to your product?   Yes   No

Do you have a concise (yet comprehensive) competitive
analysis of your product?   Yes   No

GOALS AND OBJECTIVES

Can you articulate a long-term goal for your products?   Yes   No

Do your annual objectives indicate what you want to
accomplish this year to move closer to your long-term goals?   Yes   No

Are your objectives SMART?   Yes   No

STRATEGIES AND TACTICS

Do your strategies and tactics explain how you will move
from where you are now to where your objectives specify
you want to go?   Yes   No

Do they make sense given your environmental scan?   Yes   No

PLANNING CHECKLIST, *continued*

IMPLEMENTATION

Does your plan specify the people and resources necessary
to act on the strategies and tactics?   Yes   No

Have you obtained commitment from the principal parties
involved in implementation?   Yes   No

TRACKING

Have you specified measures and milestones to monitor
progress toward accomplishing the objectives?   Yes   No

4   Market Research

"Because we are bound by what we know, it is difficult to imagine what we don't know."

—Walter Wriston,
former Citicorp president

In order to obtain the data for an environmental scan, you must collect information on both the market and competitors. Best-practices companies maintain a knowledge book on relevant information for their businesses to create *institutional memory.*[1] Product managers are responsible for creating and maintaining a fact book for their area of responsibility that provides similar information.[2] Quite a bit can be obtained informally through the grapevine—salespeople, trade shows, and other human sources. Even though this may be an informal network, it is absolutely critical for managers and requires care and nurturing.

Create a Source Network

For most B2B (business-to-business) product managers, as well as many consumer product managers, the sales force and channel members provide a significant amount of research data—what customers want, what competitors are doing, what changes are emerging. The data influx is erratic and unpredictable,

---

1. For more information on this point, refer to Robert Duboff and Jim Spaeth, *Market Research Matters* (New York: John Wiley & Sons, 2000) p. 96.

2. For more information on the product fact book, refer to Linda Gorchels, *The Product Manager's Handbook* (Chicago: NTC Business Books, 2000) p. 134.

so improving the process can be to the product manager's benefit. It's useful to learn about the call reports and other reports salespeople submit to corporate and determine whether competitive and market feedback can be built in. Salespeople will be more motivated to supply data if they perceive value from the process (e.g., sharing information across territories will provide ideas beneficial in closing sales) and/or if they are recognized for their contributions (perhaps at annual sales meetings).

Industry analysts and people from the relevant business press can shed light on external trends and competitive maneuvers. Lead users may be another source of trend data, especially with regard to new products. (More information on lead user research is contained in Chapter 8.) Consequently, product managers should strive to build a network of these experts to tap into when gathering "intelligence" for a plan or a business decision.

Foundational Step: Create and Maintain a Network of Informal Sources

Have you identified the people sources (industry analysts, lead users, key customers, salespeople, distributors) who have concrete knowledge about your industry, products, and customers? Do you maintain regular contact with them? Have you established a mutually beneficial information exchange process?

Formulate the Research Problem

Beyond the informal networks, product managers need a basic familiarity with formal research. The formal research can be primary or secondary, qualitative or quantitative. *Primary research* refers to the process of designing a project to gather information about a specific problem or issue. *Secondary research* refers to the process of collecting information that was not specifically gathered for the research issue. Searching online and library sources, for example, would be secondary research. *Quantitative research* refers to numeric data (percentages, means, etc.) obtained from a relatively large probability sample with the intent of projecting it to the population from which the sample was drawn. *Qualitative research* refers to the deeper, more subjective information that is gathered from a smaller sample. Case studies and focus groups generally provide qualitative research. The steps in the research process are shown in Figure 4.1.

The process starts by stating the marketing or management question as concisely as possible, with an action-oriented perspective. The true value of research

FIGURE 4.1 *The Marketing Research Process*

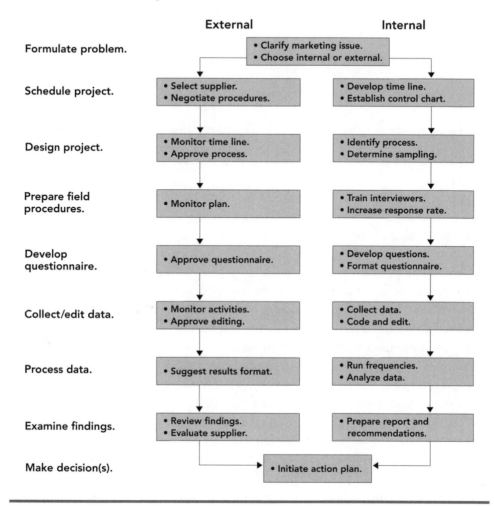

comes from what it helps you *do*—not just what it helps you *know*—and the problem statement should reflect this. For example, rather than simply saying you are going to research pricing, state the problem as: "should we increase price, and if so, by how much?" Next, provide evidence that the issue merits sufficient importance to commission research. Evidence could come from many sources. Unit sales began to decline when a competitor lowered its price. The sales force lost-order reports point to a potential pricing problem. Finally, indicate the specific spin-off questions, along with possible research approaches to addressing the questions.

SPIN-OFF QUESTIONS ————————→	RESEARCH APPROACH
Have customers been price sensitive in the past?	Examine sales records to estimate price sensitivity to past changes.
Does it vary by segment?	Compare profiles of customers who, in the past, exhibited the most and least price sensitivity.
How strong is customer loyalty?	Analyze customer records to assess length of patronage.

Figure 4.2 contains a worksheet to help you think through a comprehensive look at relating a marketing issue to a marketing research process. Additional ideas on defining the problem are contained in Figure 4.3, the marketing research idea starter.

Part of the problem formulation involves estimating the requirements of the total project. When is a final answer to these questions necessary? Work back from the date the final report is due to determine timing. When does data collection need to be completed? When do interviewers need to be hired and trained? When does the questionnaire need to be finalized? Then ask whether you have the time, skills, and resources to do the job internally or whether the work should be contracted out. If it is necessary to go outside, issue a written request for proposal (RFP) that specifies the topic, specific skills, deadlines, and business matters such as payment, confidentiality, rights to the raw data, and so on.

Formulating the research definition also involves secondary research. What trade association offerings help you better understand the problem? Does your company have any prior research in the files that can assist in this evaluatory phase? Are there any government statistics that suggest trends or leading indicators that might be appropriate? The secondary data are important for a number of reasons. They help you better define the problem, suggest potential improvements in methodology, and provide comparative data. However, you must exercise some caution as well. It's important to assess how well the general data "fit" the requirements of your specific issue. If the secondary research was conducted for a different industry or market segment, it may need to be adapted to fit your needs. In addition, you should consider the purpose of the publication to evaluate the possibility of bias. Political, civic, religious, and trade organizations may knowingly or unknowingly slant the findings. And finally, you should study the information for evidence of quality. Were the questions correctly worded? Was

---

FIGURE 4.2 *Research Problem Definition Worksheet*

Marketing issue: _____

Evidence:

   1. _____

   2. _____

   3. _____

Spin-off questions: ————————————▶   Research approach:

   _____   _____

   _____   _____

   _____   _____

   _____   _____

---

the appropriate methodology used? Are there any conceptual errors in the written report or article? Secondary data can help provide the type of information contained in the worksheet in Figure 4.4.

Step One: Clearly Define the Research Issue

Do you have a clear statement of the marketing issue, spin-off questions, and related research approaches? Is the focus on what you are going to *do* (in addition to what you want to know)? Have you carefully examined secondary data prior to jumping into primary research? What do you already know? Can a decision be made without the expense of additional research? Do you need a snapshot of current circumstances or a longitudinal study (over time)? What is the risk of a wrong decision? Is the research being planned to justify a decision already made? (If so, don't do the research!) Do you have the internal expertise and resources to conduct the research? What research and analysis can be done internally and which parts can be done externally?

FIGURE 4.3 *Marketing Research Idea Starter*

Example Issues for Marketing Planning

STAGE OF PLANNING PROCESS	TYPES OF QUESTIONS TO ADDRESS	EXAMPLE SOURCES/ TECHNIQUES
Environmental Scan		
Business assessment	• What are the short- and long-term goals, mission, and objectives? • What is our corporate image among present customers? Potential customers? Distribution channel members?	• Internal documents • Sales force input • Focus groups and surveys • Intranet survey
Market analysis	• What is the size and growth rate of the total market? • What segments exist? • What new markets are likely to open up? • What are the key buying influences affecting the sale of the product category? • What brands are preferred? At what prices? Why? • How much of these markets have we penetrated and why? What is our current and projected market share? • How are our best customers different from our periodic customers?	• Census data • Industry trade publication research departments • Trade association reports • Customer sales records matched with market demographics • Customer satisfaction research • Customer letters and complaints • Internal records databased for easy manipulation • Cluster-based segmentation

FIGURE 4.3 *Marketing Research Idea Starter*, continued

Example Issues for Marketing Planning

STAGE OF PLANNING PROCESS	TYPES OF QUESTIONS TO ADDRESS	EXAMPLE SOURCES/ TECHNIQUES
	• How loyal are our customers?	
Competitive analysis	• Who are our top competitors? For which products, markets, regions? • What image does the market have of the competitors? • What are the strengths and weaknesses of the competitors? • What are the apparent strategies of the competitors?	• Competitive intelligence • Spreadsheet analysis of specific strategy components • Benchmarking • Website research
Performance history	• What has been the three-year sales trend (in units and dollars) of the product line? Compared to the industry? Compared to the plan? • What features/benefits of your product are distinguishable and important? • What has been the customer and competitor reaction to pricing?	• Internal records • Brand reputation studies • Customer satisfaction research (longitudinal research) • Warranty claims analysis • Benchmarking

FIGURE 4.3 *Marketing Research Idea Starter,* continued

Example Issues for Marketing Planning

STAGE OF PLANNING PROCESS	TYPES OF QUESTIONS TO ADDRESS	EXAMPLE SOURCES/ TECHNIQUES
Environmental Scan, *continued*		
	• What advertising approaches have or have not worked? • What is the current level of awareness? • What is the satisfaction level of the trade? • What is the satisfaction level of end customers? (Timeliness; shipment accuracy; complaints; financing; warranty support)	
Trend dynamics	• What technological changes are likely? How might they impact your sales? • What have been the industry trends? • What economic or social trends exist that could impact sales?	• Clipping services • Trade publications • Panel data • Longitudinal data • Customized E-mail services
Synthesis		
Sales forecast	• What have been the historical sales patterns? • What are the expected sales based on managerial input?	• Time series analysis • Compiled forecasts using inputs from sales force, management team, and other experts

FIGURE 4.3 *Marketing Research Idea Starter,* continued

Example Issues for Marketing Planning

STAGE OF PLANNING PROCESS	TYPES OF QUESTIONS TO ADDRESS	EXAMPLE SOURCES/ TECHNIQUES
	• What leading indicators exist and how do they relate to our sales?	• Regression analyses using selected leading indicators and/or strategic inputs
Positioning statement	• How is our product/ company perceived by the customers relative to the competition? How would we like it to be perceived?	• Perceptual mapping
Action Plan		
Product strategy	• What line extensions should be added? What can be done to reduce "cannibalization?" • What new uses/ applications exist for our product? • What new product ideas can we develop? • What is the customer reaction to new product concepts? • Is the marketing strategy right for the new product?	• TURF analysis for line extensions • Customer visit programs • Focus groups • Goals segmentation research • Concept testing • Market testing

FIGURE 4.3 *Marketing Research Idea Starter,* continued

Example Issues for Marketing Planning

STAGE OF PLANNING PROCESS	TYPES OF QUESTIONS TO ADDRESS	EXAMPLE SOURCES/ TECHNIQUES
Action Plan, *continued*		
Pricing strategy	• Which of two (or more) product/price combinations should be used? • How can we increase the perceived value to the customer?	• Trade-off analysis • Research on the importance and perceived competitive performance of product features
Promotional strategy	• What message are we communicating to customers? • Which of two (or more) ads, mail lists, Web pages, etc., is more effective?	• Attitude/attitude change • Copy testing (pretests) • Recall testing • Split-testing
Distribution strategy	• What information can I obtain about the end user? • How satisfied are our distributors? Reps? Suppliers?	• POS (point-of-sale) program data • Satisfaction research among channel members

FIGURE 4.4 *Market Analysis*

DIVISION		GROUP		PRODUCT LINE						MARKET				
				Total industry sales volume		Total industry revenue		Average industry revenue		Product sales volume		Product sales revenue		Average revenue
Customer demo-graphic categories	Number of industry purchasers	Customers as % of industry	% company product volume	Units	%	$	%			Units	%	$	%	
Total		100%	100%		100%	$	100%	$			100%	$	100%	$

Design and Schedule the Project

After the research issue is defined, the next step is designing and scheduling the project. These are overlapping rather than sequential steps. The type of survey methodology must now be selected. Although focus groups, experiments, and market tests are important marketing research techniques, the primary emphasis in this chapter will be on surveys. Mail surveys may be appropriate for quantitative research. Personal surveys lend themselves to qualitative research. Telephone and E-mail could combine the two, as long as appropriate sample control is exercised. A comparison of the techniques is presented in Figure 4.5. Some advantages and disadvantages are shared by all survey approaches. Currently, response rates are declining for surveys, regardless of the methodology used, and all methodologies can benefit from multiple contacts and incentives. The table in Figure 4.5 focuses primarily on differences.

Sample selection is part of the research design. From what population do you want information? Should you be talking to current customers, former customers, or noncustomers? Are companies of a certain size or industry more important than others? Remember that sample data can only be projected back to the population from which the sample was drawn. In other words, a sample drawn from one industry, in general, should not be projected to another industry, and a sample from one geographic region should not be projected to a different region—at least not without recognition of the fact that differences may exist. Unfortunately, many people select samples without giving thought to the relationship between the sample and the population of interest.

Sample size is another important consideration. In general, if you are conducting qualitative research, relatively small, nonprobability samples may be appropriate. If you are conducting quantitative research, larger probability samples are necessary. The size of the sample depends on the variability in the population. If you are selecting a sample from a homogeneous population, smaller samples may suffice. As the amount of heterogeneity increases, so must the sample size.

Steps Two and Three: Design and Schedule the Project

Have you matched the type of survey to the type of data required? Have you carefully articulated the profile of desired respondents (i.e., the population)? Is the size of the sample large enough given the variability in the population?

FIGURE 4.5 *Comparison of Survey Approaches*

	MAIL	E-MAIL	TELEPHONE	PERSONAL
Advantages				
	• Useful for potentially sensitive questions • Greater perception of confidentiality or anonymity	• Fastest potential responses • Best for short surveys	• Fast response • Can blend open and closed questions • Best for short surveys	• Potential rapport building • Useful for complex questions
Disadvantages				
	• Perceived as "junk mail" • Slow • Potential question sequence bias	• Easily deleted • Perceived as "junk E-mail" • Not all potential respondents have E-mail	• Increasing phone numbers dedicated to fax, computer • Answering machines/voice mail; caller ID; call blocking • Somewhat labor intensive	• Labor intensive • Potential interviewer bias
Ways to Increase Effectiveness				
	Split-sequence mailings	Careful wording of the subject line in the header	Calling at staggered times	Using trade shows and similar groupings to reduce costs

Prepare Field Procedures

Once the research methodology is determined, it is time to prepare the field procedures. Lists of potential respondents (i.e., the sampling frame) may need to be acquired for mail, E-mail, or telephone surveys, and interviewers may need to be hired and/or trained for phone and personal surveys.

Product managers are frequently involved in the selection or development of the sampling frame. (This will be true for both focus groups and surveys.) If the "wrong" respondents participate in the research, the resulting information will not satisfy the project requirements. If you sell through distributors and desire to survey end users, obtaining a list of appropriate names can be a challenge. It may be necessary to work with a list broker or direct marketing agency to select the best-fit list available. The Direct Marketing Association (the-dma.org) and the Standard Rate and Data Service guides (srds.com) may be useful idea sources in this effort. Similarly, if the response rate is too low, results can be misleading. Therefore, multiple contacts should be built into the budget to encourage responses.

When interviewers are part of the field procedures, careful monitoring is necessary to be sure the information is collected without bias. Field workers should be provided instructional data, such as the following:

- what the survey is about
- when the survey is to start and end
- how to select respondents
- how to initiate interviews and build rapport
- how each question should be asked and in what order
- how to choose methods of probing, encouraging responses, and aiding memory
- how each questionnaire is to be examined
- what to do with the completed questionnaires
- when and how the interviewer will be paid

Step Four: Prepare Field Procedures

Do you have a solid list of names, mail, and E-mail addresses, and/or phone numbers to draw a sample from? Is this list reflective of the group (i.e., population) you want to research? Have you incorporated incentives and the ability/time to contact potential respondents more than once to increase the response rate? If you are conducting phone or personal surveys, have the interviewers been trained? Have you built in quality controls?

Develop Questionnaire

Developing the questionnaire actually involves several components: (a) cover letter; (b) instructions; (c) question content, wording, response format, sequence; (d) classification data; and (e) closing. In addition, this step doesn't end until the data collection instrument has been pretested and modified.

Cover Letter

The cover letter makes the first impression and should be professional, friendly, and motivate the individual to respond. It should explain how the recipient was selected, the importance of the sponsor and the research project, and the role of confidentiality or anonymity. In addition, it should cover administrative issues such as how to return the questionnaire (a stamped reply envelope should be included, even if fax return is an option), timing (if relevant), and an explanation of any related incentive.

Instructions

Although many questionnaires are self-explanatory, instructions are often necessary. They should be as concise as possible and clearly distinguished from the questions. If examples are used to explain how to answer the questions, care must be taken to avoid bias.

Questions

The content of the questions should obviously reflect the research purpose. Strive to avoid questions that do not relate directly to the stated purpose and are simply nice to have answers to. Remember that each additional question adds to the length of the survey and thereby has the potential to discourage recipients from responding. Sometimes filter questions (e.g., have you used the product within the past year) are necessary to validate or interpret subsequent responses.

The wording of the question should be clear and free of bias. Sometimes two questions are preferred to one if that improves clarity or specificity of response. For example, if a question asked respondents to rate a firm's quality and friendliness, it is possible that the respondent could rate quality differently from friendliness. Two separate questions would be better. You must decide whether the question should be open-ended (with no response categories) or closed-ended. Open-ended questions are appropriate for qualitative research and, if used appropriately, can stimulate in-depth responses. Closed-ended questions are appropriate for quantitative research and are more easily put into a database for analysis. However, the response categories for closed-ended questions must be carefully planned.

Most research texts recommend that response categories be "mutually exclusive and collectively exhaustive," which simply means that the responses should incorporate all possible answers and not leave any out. Response categories of 10–20 and 20–30 are not mutually exclusive since 20 is contained in both categories, and the two categories are not collectively exhaustive since less than 10 and more than 30 are not options. From a practical perspective, this implies that "don't know," "not applicable," and "other" are responses that should be part of many multiple-choice questions.

There are many thoughts about the sequence of questions. A common approach is the funnel approach, which implies starting with broad questions and progressively narrowing the focus. There should be simple, interesting questions at the beginning, with more difficult or sensitive questions later in the survey when respondents are already involved. The flow of questions should be logical, with questions of similar content, instructions, or response scales grouped together. Sometimes it is not clear whether the answer to one question may affect the answer to later questions. When that is the case, several versions of the questionnaire may be mailed out with the same questions in a different sequence to balance this effect.

Classification Data

Demographic classification data should be included in the questionnaire to allow cross-tabulation of results. Were certain types of respondents more apt to answer questions one way while another group answered differently? The response categories for the demographic data should mirror response categories from any published sources you might want to use to project the information. For example, if you want to project responses to certain census categories, the question responses must contain the same categories as the census records.

Closing

The end of the questionnaire should provide an appropriate closing. Thank the respondents for their time in completing the questionnaire, remind them of the incentive (gift), and encourage them to return the completed study.

Pretest

The final element of questionnaire design is the pretest—administering the final questionnaire to potential respondents to assess their ability to complete it accurately and to determine whether rewording or different questions are necessary. The pretest or pilot serves the same purpose as the beta test in new product development. It assesses how the instrument performs under the actual conditions of data collection.

Step Five: Develop the Questionnaire

Do you have a cover letter that is both professional in appearance and serves to motivate respondents? Are clear instructions built into the questionnaire? Is each question necessary, sufficient, and appropriate for the research study? Is the wording free from bias? Do the responses include all possible answers without overlap? Is the sequence of questions logical? Are similar questions grouped together appropriately? Do you include demographic questions? Have you pretested the questionnaire?

Collect, Edit, and Code Data

After the questionnaire has been pretested, data collection can begin in earnest. For postal surveys it's a matter of getting the questionnaires in the mail and waiting for returns. For surveys requiring interviewers, systems must be established to ensure appropriate callbacks and quality control. Periodic checks of the completed questionnaires should take place to identify and correct any interviewer errors or bias as soon as possible.

Editing and coding are the next steps in the process. *Editing* refers to the process of scanning the data collection forms to ensure they are complete and consistent and that the instructions were followed. Decisions need to be made on how to handle questionnaires that have potential problems. For example, if answers to two questions contradict each other, the researcher must decide whether to eliminate the responses to those two questions or to eliminate the entire questionnaire. If it appears that a respondent has used response scales incorrectly (e.g., "1" was used as high whereas "5" should have been used), the researcher must again determine whether to change the scoring of those questions or eliminate the questionnaire. If editing is not done (or done improperly), the resulting data used for analysis will yield inaccurate results.

Coding is the process of assigning numbers to question responses so that they can be analyzed mathematically. For most closed-ended (e.g., multiple choice and scaled rating) questions, the codes are already part of the data collection form. For open-ended questions, on the other hand, it may be necessary to categorize the results and assign a code to each category. If similar prior research has been done, check these prior studies for established codes. Be sure to code ideas rather than words and accept the fact that some written responses may require more than one code. Limit the number of codes to a manageable number for subsequent analysis. Product managers may be involved in creating a codebook where all information about the codes is recorded.

The final aspect of this part of the process is entering the data into a relevant computer program. For small surveys, an electronic spreadsheet (e.g., Excel) may suffice. For larger studies, a statistical database (e.g., SPSS) would be preferred.

Step Six: Collect, Edit, and Code Data

Do you have quality control checkpoints built into the data collection process? Are the forms edited before being input into any computer program? Has a codebook been established to assign categorical codes to written responses to facilitate cross-tabulation and other analysis? Has the information been input into a relevant computer program?

Process Data and Make Decisions

Analyzing the results of the research is finally at hand. The starting point should be a simple tabulation of responses (i.e., frequency counts) to check for outliers or possible missed errors. Beyond that, the type of analysis depends on the type of question. The major types of response measurements used in marketing research are nominal, ordinal, and interval scaled responses.

Nominal responses are merely names of categories. Male versus female and user versus nonuser, for example, are nominal categories. The information is generally analyzed in terms of percentages.

Ordinal responses are also categories, but with order implied. Good, better, and best is an ordinal scale since there is value implied with the categories. "Best" is better than "better," and "better" is better than "good." However, if the numbers 1, 2, and 3 were assigned to the categories, it would not be appropriate to calculate a mean response.

Interval responses are more precise than ordinal responses, with categories of equal intervals, thereby enabling the calculation of a mean. For example, if respondents are asked to rate something on a 1-to-5 scale, the presumption is that the difference between 1 and 2 is the same as the difference between 2 and 3, between 3 and 4, and between 4 and 5. In other words, there is the same interval between categories. (Note: there is an additional type of scale, a ratio scale, that requires an absolute zero and is more appropriate for scientific research than for marketing research.)

The type of scale used becomes important to determine appropriate statistical techniques when cross-tabulating questions. For example, if a goal of the research is to determine whether users and nonusers have different attitudes toward a particular product or issue, the fact that user/nonuser is a nominal scale may limit the analysis used to chi-square or ANOVA. On the other hand, if two interval scaled questions (e.g., advertising expenditures and sales) are to be compared, it may be possible to use linear regression. The important point to remember is that the type of responses built into the design of the questionnaire will affect the type of statistical analysis possible after the data are collected.

The final activity is to make a decision. If a decision is not possible at this point, the research has not accomplished its objective.

Step Seven: Process Data and Make Decisions

Have you run a simple tabulation of the survey responses to uncover random errors in data entry or unusual responses not caught during the edit phase? Are you using statistical techniques appropriate for the type of question(s)? Have you thoughtfully evaluated the results in an effort to recommend a decision?

KEY POINTS

- Establish and maintain contact with select salespeople, industry analysts, and other individuals who can provide market and competitive insight.
- State research problems in terms of what you are going to *do* with (as well as know from) the results.
- Plan multiple contacts, if possible, to increase response rates.
- Remember that sample results can be projected only to the population from which the sample was drawn.
- Carefully train interviewers to minimize bias.
- Develop the questionnaire to encourage honest and active participation without introducing bias.
- Pretest the questionnaire before full-scale administration.
- Build quality control checkpoints into the data collection, editing, and coding process.
- Analyze data by referring back to the initial objectives of the research process.

SURVEY CHECKLIST

MARKETING PLANNING ISSUES

Can you make the decision without doing any research?	Yes	No
Do you have the abilities and skills to handle it internally?	Yes	No
If you need help, have you evaluated possible suppliers?	Yes	No
Do you have a concise problem definition?	Yes	No
Have you established a time line for the research?	Yes	No

RESEARCH DESIGN ISSUES

Have you determined whether you need qualitative or quantitative data?	Yes	No
Will you need input from different types of research designs?	Yes	No
Is your research design consistent with the required time frame?	Yes	No

SURVEY DESIGN ISSUES

Have you compared telephone, mail, personal, and E-mail alternatives to determine which is the most appropriate for your needs?	Yes	No
Have you selected the appropriate population and sample?	Yes	No
Is your sample large enough to accomplish your goals?	Yes	No
Did you build more than one contact into your time line and budget?	Yes	No
If you are using interviewers, have they been trained?	Yes	No
Did you build response incentives into your budget?	Yes	No

SURVEY CHECKLIST, *continued*

QUESTIONNAIRE ISSUES

If using mail, do you have an acceptable cover letter?	Yes	No
Do your questions encourage honest, thoughtful responses?	Yes	No
Do you have clear instructions for the respondent?	Yes	No
Will answers to the questions allow you to discriminate between respondents?	Yes	No
Is each question a single question?	Yes	No
Are the questions free of bias?	Yes	No
Does the layout look attractive and easy to complete?	Yes	No
Have you pretested the questionnaire?	Yes	No
Did you include demographic questions?	Yes	No
Did you thank respondents in your close?	Yes	No

DATA ANALYSIS ISSUES

Have you edited the questionnaires for quality?	Yes	No
Did you develop a codebook for open-ended questions?	Yes	No
Were all questionnaires coded prior to data entry?	Yes	No
Has data entry been checked for accuracy?	Yes	No
Have you identified nominal, ordinal, and interval categories of questions to ensure use of appropriate statistical techniques?	Yes	No
Did you incorporate appropriate visuals for your audience?	Yes	No

Financial Foundations
of Planning

*"We didn't actually overspend our budget. The allocation simply fell
short of our expenditure."*

—Keith Davis, business author

P roduct managers may operate as cost-recovery centers, revenue centers, or profit centers, depending
on the expectations of the organization. Never-
theless, for most product managers, profit is an expected outcome or result of
strategic direction, even if the short-term goal on a marketing plan doesn't specifically identify profit. A basic understanding of the finance function is therefore
important. Even experienced product managers are sometimes not quite sure
why they are doing what they are doing in terms of financial management. Yet
the ability to present a business case (be it for an annual budget approval or for
a new product) and discuss it with financial management is almost a prerequisite
to survival.

The two most relevant financial statements for product managers are the
income (or profit-and-loss, i.e., P&L) statement and the balance sheet. Most product managers will have some type of P&L for their products, and some will have
balance sheets. The income statement lists the revenues and expenses associated
with a firm, a business unit, a product line, or a product manager over a period
of time such as a fiscal year. An example of the linkages among company, product manager, and product income statements is shown in Figure 5.1. The balance
sheet is a snapshot of a firm's assets, liabilities, and equities at a point in time.
Without outside capital, the difference in the balance sheet between fiscal years is
due to the related income statement. This is presented graphically as follows:

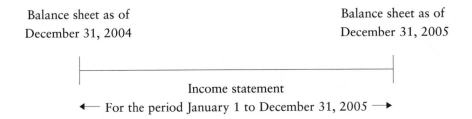

Product managers should establish a framework of financial plans, budgets, and controls to improve the long-term financial performance of their products and services as they relate to overall company performance. The two primary categories of financial tools are those used to evaluate product line profitability (flexible product budgets and product costing) and those used to weigh investment alternatives.

Evaluating Product Lines

Fixed costs are those that do not change (in total) for a given time or activity. These costs are also referred to as the cost of *being in* business. Since the total cost remains constant, the cost per unit goes down as volume increases. Variable costs are those directly related to a given activity and are sometimes referred to as the cost of *doing business*. Since the per-unit cost stays essentially the same, the total increases as volume goes up. Semi-variable or semi-fixed costs have components of each. To the extent possible, separating out the fixed and variable components allows them to be analyzed more carefully in a product budget. In addition, as will be discussed later, some costs are *common costs* that may be difficult to link directly to specific products or product managers. Knowledge of the fixed and variable costs allows a product manager to calculate contribution margin and breakeven.

The *contribution margin* on a product is that amount of price that contributes to fixed costs (if sales are below breakeven) or to profit (if sales are beyond breakeven). Unit contribution margin is the difference between selling price and variable costs per unit. If a product is priced at $80, with a variable cost of $30, each unit sold will contribute $50 to either fixed costs or profit. Whether it contributes to fixed costs or profit depends on whether the unit sales exceed the break-even point.

The *break-even point* is calculated by dividing total fixed costs by unit contribution margin. If fixed costs in the previous example are $150,000, the break-even point would be 3,000 units ($150,000 ÷ $50). If a target profit of $50,000

FIGURE 5.1 *Comparison of Firm, Product Manager,*
Product, and Customer Income Statements

Comparison of Income Statement Components

	Total Company	Product Manager 1	Product Manager 2
Sales	$900,000	$500,000	$400,000
Variable expenses			
cost of goods sold	400,000	270,000	130,000
other variable expenses	100,000	70,000	30,000
Total variable expenses	500,000	340,000	160,000
Contribution margin	400,000	160,000	240,000
less direct fixed expenses	150,000	80,000	70,000
Product manager margins	250,000	$80,000	$170,000
less common fixed expenses	160,000		
Net income	$90,000		

	Product Manager 2	Standard Model	Custom Model
Sales	$400,000	$150,000	$250,000
Variable expenses			
cost of goods sold	130,000	50,000	80,000
other variable expenses	30,000	20,000	10,000
Total variable expenses	160,000	70,000	90,000
Contribution margin	240,000	80,000	160,000
less direct product expenses	30,000	10,000	20,000
Product margins	210,000	$70,000	$140,000
less common fixed expenses	40,000		
Net income	$170,000		

FIGURE 5.1 *Comparison of Firm, Product Manager,*
           Product, and Customer Income Statements, continued

	Custom Model	Contractors	Residential
Sales	$250,000	$180,000	$70,000
Variable expenses			
cost of goods sold	80,000	60,000	20,000
other variable expenses	10,000	3,000	7,000
Total variable expenses	90,000	63,000	27,000
Contribution margin	160,000	117,000	43,000
less direct market expenses	10,000	7,000	3,000
Customer segment margins	150,000	$110,000	$40,000
less common fixed expenses	10,000		
Net income	$140,000		

is added to the fixed costs in the numerator, the target sales volume (i.e., sales goal) would be 4,000 units ($200,000 ÷ $50).

Step One: Clarify the Types of Costs Associated with Your Product Line

Define your products' variable and fixed cost components. Develop appropriate contribution income statements with this information. Calculate the contribution margin(s). Assess whether current sales exceed breakeven or target sales volume.

Flexible Product Budgets

Product budgets are an essential aspect of the product manager planning and control process. Most product budgets are variations of a standard income or profit-and-loss statement, but with emphasis on forecasted revenues and costs as appropriate for the product manager's area of responsibility. The budget can be developed by product, by customer, by market, by territory, or by any categorization process relevant to improved decision making. In addition, there may be separate budgets for a specific new product development effort, a sales training session, or for other product-related projects. The overall product budget for a given fiscal year, therefore, should be consistent with both a two- to five-year strategic financial plan for the product(s) and with the individual project budgets for the product manager.

Whether the budget is aggressive or conservative depends on the financial management philosophy of the company. If the company takes an aggressive approach, budgets tend toward best-case situations, with the product manager expected to achieve budgeted figures. If the company takes a conservative approach, budgets tend toward worst-case situations, with the product manager expected to exceed budgeted figures.

The product budget starts with an estimate of revenues and costs (ideally developed jointly by product managers, finance, operations, and other relevant functional areas). The revenue forecast consists of an expected price multiplied by an expected number of sales units. A deviation from plan in either will result in a variance to the budget. The cost information will depend on whether costs are fixed or variable and the internal attitude toward allocations. Cost deviations will also result in budget variations. The more a product manager understands the root elements of budget variances, the greater the ability to take corrective action.

Let's take an example of a product with budgeted revenue of $50,000 and budgeted profit of $10,000. If the actual revenue and profit are $55,000 and $10,500, respectively, has performance been satisfactory? To answer the question, we need more information.

Assumptions: unit price = $50

variable cost/unit = $20

fixed costs = $20,000

forecasted sales = 1,000 units

Based on the above assumptions, the budget for the product is:

Sales ($50 × 1,000 units)	$50,000
Variable costs ($20 × 1,000 units)	20,000
Contribution margin	30,000
Fixed costs	20,000
Pretax profit	$10,000

To determine whether the "actuals" indicate adequate performance, it's useful to prepare a base budget and flexible budget using the actual sales number, and then compare the flexible budget column with the actuals. This is demonstrated in the following table:

	BUDGET STANDARDS	BASE BUDGET	FLEXIBLE BUDGET	ACTUAL	VARIANCE
		1,000	1,100	1,100	100
Sales	$50	$50,000	$55,000	$55,000	0
Variable costs	$20	$20,000	$22,000	$24,500	$2,500
Contribution	$30	$30,000	$33,000	$30,500	$−2,500
Fixed costs	$20,000	$20,000	$20,000	$20,000	0
Operating profit		$10,000	$13,000	$10,500	$−2,500

Note that the example here is built on the assumption that the variable cost is $20/unit and fixed costs are $20,000. If actual sales are 1,100 units rather than 1,000 units, variable costs should be $22,000 ($20 × 1,100 units), yielding a budgeted profit of $13,000. The actual profit of $10,500 was $2,500 less than the amount expected at a sales volume of 1,100 units. The variance column indicates that even though we were effective in exceeding the objectives (100 more units and $500 more profit than in the base budget), we were inefficient in that the variable costs were higher than anticipated.

Step Two: Develop Standards for a Flexible Budget

What are the per-unit sales, variable cost, and contribution figures that should be used in the development of your budget? (If you are responsible for a service, the unit could be an hour of service, a customer, or another variable appropriate for your situation.)

Although the variance here was in the variable cost amount, product managers should also examine variance in terms of sales data. To accomplish this, they must work with their various internal colleagues to identify the appropriate standards to use in the budgeting process. What is the best unit of sales to use— a box, case, or a pallet? Should the sale be recorded when the product is shipped or when payment is received? Should the type of sale be classified by customer, by region, by order size, by terms of sale, or by multiple variables (e.g., all of the criteria)? Is one format sufficient, or should different budgets be developed for the different units? Should the information be compared with historical results, current results from another product, or specific goals and objectives? How much detail is necessary, and when does the amount of detail become overwhelming to the point of losing its value in decision making?

Step Three: Determine the Best Sales Categories to Study for Variances in Performance in the Product Budget

What information, if available, would most improve your decision-making ability as a product manager? Can this data be used to enrich your previous budget standards? How can this information be converted to ratios (e.g., cost per shipment) that can be tracked over time to highlight changes that might require corrective action?

Product Costing

In the preceding example, there was a variance between the average product cost achieved versus cost budgeted. But how do companies determine the average product cost to use as the standard cost in a budget? Many companies use a full costing or absorption costing approach to fully allocate manufacturing "burden" to products. This is consistent with financial reporting requirements. Traditional accounting systems were designed primarily to meet the needs of investors, lenders, and tax authorities, and were built on an absorption costing approach that doesn't lend itself to product decisions. This traditional approach is based on the assumption that products should absorb not only their direct material and labor costs, but also the manufacturing overhead costs associated with products.

Companies that use a full costing or absorption costing approach sometimes hide the true contribution of a product, product line, or product manager. The cost profile of many businesses has changed with the trend to more automation and computerization. As the percentage of cost related to raw materials goes down and the percentage attributable to fixed costs goes up, the relative impact of varying production levels is magnified. Although product managers need to contribute to corporate overhead for a company to stay in business, full cost allocation (without separating out fixed costs) reduces the ability of product managers to identify causes of budget variations and thereby take corrective steps. Bad or misleading information on product costs leads to bad product decisions.

In working with finance and accounting departments, product managers should obtain product cost information in a form useful for decision making. Take an example of three products, X, Y, and Z, with per-unit raw materials costs of $45, $40, and $25, respectively. Assume manufacturing overhead is $9,000 for a given period, and the allocations are based simply on units of production. If there are 100 units of each product produced (for a total of 300 units), the costs are as follows:

	X	Y	Z
Raw materials	$45	$40	$25
Overhead ($9,000 ÷ 300)	$30	$30	$30
Total standard cost per unit	$75	$70	$55

When there is unused capacity, the products have to absorb more fixed costs. If there are only 50 units of each product produced, each one has to absorb more overhead, as shown in the following:

	X	Y	Z
Raw materials	$45	$40	$25
Overhead ($9,000 ÷ 150)	$60	$60	$60
Total standard cost per unit	$105	$100	$85

Note that the standard cost of these products suggests that the smaller volume costs $30 more per unit, rather than indicating possible unused capacity. Idle capacity should be considered a cost of the period rather than a cost of the product. If stated cost per unit fluctuates with production volume, it can be difficult to make sound pricing and marketing decisions. This type of information can sometimes lead to what is referred to as the "death spiral." Product managers attempt to raise the price to improve profitability, further compressing market demand, and thereby causing the decline to escalate.

To make better decisions, it is useful to separate out the fixed costs and use some type of direct costing or activity-based costing (ABC) analysis. These are methods of cost allocations that attempt to improve on the "arbitrary and capricious" allocation methods of financial accounting. Both attempt to assign costs to the entity (product, department, unit, etc.) causing the costs to happen, but they are used under somewhat different circumstances and use somewhat different methodological approaches. Separating out the fixed costs ideally results in more stable unit product costs as well as identifies unused capacity.[1]

Direct material and direct labor are direct costs that are materially linked to the production of specific products. However, there are other costs that could be directly linked to a product. If an inspector spends 50 percent of his or her time in monitoring a product, 50 percent of the salary might appropriately be direct costed. If a technical support person is assigned to a specific product, the entire salary might be assigned to the product. If a firm attends a trade show to equally promote 10 products, each product might be allocated 10 percent of the total costs.

As overhead costs have grown and are shared across numerous products and product managers, some companies have added activity-based costing as a complement to direct costing. With ABC, firms attempt to determine what activities

---

1. For a further discussion of ABC, refer to Sidney Baxendale, "Activity-Based Costing for the Small Business: A Primer," *Business Horizons*, January 2001, pp. 61–68.

are caused by various products or product managers and to use that information to allocate the cost of those activities. If a significant expense category is, for example, marketing communications, and if there are significantly different efforts expended to promote some products over others, it may be unfair to allocate all costs equally, as in the case of the trade show in the preceding paragraph. In that situation it may be useful to determine an hourly rate for marketing communications services (i.e., the activity) and charge products an hourly rate based on utilization. (Note: If there are no significant differences across products, taking the step to assign costs to activities is probably unnecessarily time consuming and costs can be better allocated on a percentage basis as discussed under direct costing.)

A combination of direct and activity-based costing will likely lead to a better understanding of product line costs and, therefore, product line profitability. This information can also be used for evaluating customer and channel costs and profitability.

Let's look at an example of a company with three product lines—standard, deluxe, and custom—with the following financial information:

	STANDARD		DELUXE		CUSTOM		TOTAL
	TOTAL	**UNIT**	**TOTAL**	**UNIT**	**TOTAL**	**UNIT**	
Sales	$1,835,297	$25	$2,429,185	$50	$1,177,250	$75	$5,441,732
CGS	1,064,472	15	1,457,511	30	635,715	40	3,157,698
GM	770,825	10	971,674	20	541,535	35	2,284,034
Fixed costs	1,001,531	14	622,617	13	402,861	26	2,027,009
Profit	($230,706)	($4)	$349,057	$7	$138,674	$9	$257,025

Note that the standard product appears to be losing money, based on full cost allocation, and would be a prime candidate for elimination, or at minimum, a price increase. But obviously more analysis needs to be done on the allocated overhead before the decision can be made. The following information identified those elements of fixed costs that are costs directly related to each product. Note that the total fixed costs of $2,027,009 have not changed, but have been allocated differently. Even though all costs still need to be covered, this type of breakdown helps answer three significant questions: (1) Which costs would be eliminated and which would be shifted if the product were discontinued? (2) What is the cost floor for making short-term pricing decisions? (3) Are the costs effective in accomplishing stated goals, or should changes be made to the current activities incurring the specific costs?

	DIRECT FIXED COSTS			NONDIRECT
	STANDARD	**DELUXE**	**CUSTOM**	
Advertising	$140,053	$31,101	$0	$38,528
Sales expenses	52,431	26,567	9,889	188,701
Consulting	5,000	0	0	6,854
Credit card fees	15,466	0	0	0
Education	6,930			0
Literature	66,303	8,811	23,882	12,026
Trade shows	30,516	0	0	6,500
Other direct costs	33,522	1,702	0	
Subtotal	$350,522	$75,192	$44,038	$252,609
Total direct costs		$469,752		
Other nondirect				$1,304,648
Total nondirect				$1,557,257
Total overhead		$2,027,009		

Examining the direct costs related to each product provides better data to decide whether to eliminate the product and/or lower the price to meet the competition. If we assume the direct costs of $350,522 related to the standard product would be eliminated if we dropped the product, it would not reduce the full $1,001,531 of overhead charged to it under the fully allocated approach. The difference of $651,009 between the two would need to be reallocated to the remaining two products. If we assume the amount would be split evenly between the remaining two products ($325,504 to each), then the custom product would now show a net loss ($138,674 − $325,504 = −186,830)—and the deluxe product would be barely profitable. Therefore, before dropping a product you must determine whether the overhead costs the product absorbs would be completely eliminated or simply shifted to other products (potentially causing them to be marginal or negative performers). Even though it initially appeared that dropping the standard product might save the company $230,706 (the net loss reported on the initial income statement), the shifting of the nondirect overhead costs would make another product line negative. On the other hand, a better understanding of direct costs could also identify a losing product that appears profitable based on arbitrary allocations.

If the standard product is retained, you may need to decide about its price. Assume a competitor has brought out a competing product for $23. Should you try to match the $23 price, maintain your $25 price, or raise the price to some higher level? Part of the answer will depend on the price sensitivity of the market and the potential for waging a price war with the competitor. But in any event, knowing the direct costs of the product would be a piece of data relevant to making the decision. Expanding the preceding information into unit numbers yields the following:

| | STANDARD VERSION | |
	TOTAL	UNIT
Sales	$1,835,297	$25
Cost of goods sold	1,064,472	15
Gross margin	770,825	10
Direct costs	350,522	5
Direct contribution	420,303	5
Indirect allocated overhead	651,009	9
Net profit	($230,706)	($4)

Based on this information, the average direct unit cost of the product would be the combination of the cost of goods sold ($15) and the direct costs ($5), or $20. This would be the short-term cost floor, meaning that any units priced above $20 would have the potential to contribute to the indirect fixed costs. If it were decided to match the competitor's price of $23, each unit sold would contribute $3 to the fixed costs.

The final question listed earlier was "Are the costs effective in accomplishing stated goals, or should changes be made to the current activities incurring the specific costs?" In looking at the direct fixed costs for the standard product, advertising accounts for $140,053 of the amount. Since this is the single biggest expense category of the indirect costs, it should be examined to determine whether the advertising is accomplishing the stated goals. Similarly, the remaining costs should be examined in descending order of magnitude to determine their effectiveness. Identifying that some products are using significant amounts of a specific resource (be it advertising, machine time, or specialized labor) is the first step in determining whether these products are optimizing their use of these resources. Knowing the costs doesn't make the decision for you, but it arms you with better data to use when deciding how to react to resource constraints or a competitive threat.

Step Four: Determine Which Fixed Costs Are Directly Linked to Specific Products or Customers (as Part of Your Product Costing Initiative)

Before making decisions on product or customer changes (especially rationalization), be sure to identify which costs would actually be eliminated if the decision were made. Which costs are caused by the specific products or customers?[2]

So far the discussion has focused on past costs, but product decision making should focus on the future. As alluded to earlier, even if costs are caused by specific products, the real question a product manager needs to address is whether the costs are relevant for future decisions. For example, sunk costs result from past decisions that cannot be changed (such as, monies spent to repackage a product), and they are generally not relevant to decisions on future directions. Textbook problems and examples normally delineate between relevant and irrelevant costs. However, in practice, identifying relevant cost information can be a difficult process, primarily because historical cost data are used to predict future costs. As a result, there will always be an element of prediction error.

Predicting revenue changes that result from cost or price changes is also a best guess process based on analogous data from the past. Assume that plans are

---

2. For a good discussion of product costing, refer to Wayne J. Morse, James R. Davis, and Al L. Hartgraves, *Management Accounting, A Strategic Approach,* 2e (Mason, Ohio: South-Western College Publishing, 2000).

being developed for a product experiencing declining sales. Three mutually exclusive alternatives are being compared: (1) increasing annual promotional expenditures by $10,000; (2) raising the price by $10; or (3) reducing the price by $5. Although best-case, worst-case, and most likely outcomes could be considered for each, here we will look only at the profit impact of the most likely cases. Based on experience, the increase in advertising is expected to increase unit sales by 100, the price increase is expected to reduce unit sales by 60, and the price reduction is expected to increase unit sales by 20. The comparative data are as follows:

	CURRENT SITUATION	AD INCREASE	RAISE PRICE	REDUCE PRICE
Sales (10,000 units at $995)	$9,950,000	$10,049,500	$9,989,700	$9,919,800
CGS (10,000 units at $250)	2,500,000	2,525,000	2,485,000	2,505,000
Gross margin	7,450,000	7,524,500	7,504,700	7,414,800
Controllable expenses	2,000,000	2,010,000	2,000,000	2,000,000
Contribution margin	$5,450,000	$5,514,500	$5,504,700	$5,414,800

Of the three alternatives, the first appears to offer the greatest improvement ($64,500) over the current situation compared with the next two alternatives, offering $54,700 and –$35,200, respectively. However, other questions should be addressed. How risky are each of the alternatives? In particular, Alternative 1 involves an investment that bears further analysis. Is the expected return sufficient to justify the $10,000 investment? Could the money be better spent on some other investment? These are questions that will be explored in the next section on evaluating investment alternatives.

Step Five: Incorporate Probability and Risk into Your Product Costing Analyses

When comparing alternatives, think about the best-case, worst-case, and most likely outcomes of each alternative, as well as the probability of each occurring. Then select the alternative that provides the best posture for future profitability.

Evaluating Investment Alternatives

Product managers frequently need to make strategic comparisons of investment alternatives for new products, promotional campaigns, or other marketing-related projects. For example, marketing mix expenditures such as advertising, promotion, sales force expenditures, and so on can be viewed as projects in the sense that they are investments intended to produce some future cash flow to the firm. Thus, an increase of $1 million in advertising must be weighed against expanding the sales force or adopting a product improvement. Most will require simple cost-benefit analyses, but some (primarily new product development efforts) could require more detailed financial valuation techniques. Capital budgeting is an area of finance that deals with the prioritization of projects within a firm. Approval of these capital expenditures depends on how much future revenue will be generated and whether this revenue will exceed cost outlays by an acceptable amount. Capital budgeting equations or models are used to make the determination. Some of the most common models are payback, accounting rate of return, net present value, and internal rate of return.

Payback and accounting rate of return are models that do not consider the time value of money. This is appropriate for modest investments with minimal cash inflows required to recoup the investment. *Payback* refers to the time (in months or years) that it takes a new product or marketing project to earn enough net revenue to cover the cost of the initial investment. Management generally determines a maximum acceptable payback period, and the length of this period is used as a criterion or hurdle to evaluate such projects.

The *accounting rate of return* (often referred to as *return on investment*), determines what percent of the initial investment will be returned each year in terms of net revenue. For example, if the average annual net revenue of a new product is determined to be $15,000, and the initial investment is $100,000, the return on the initial investment is 15 percent (15,000 ÷ 100,000). A variation of this method divides the average annual profits by the average investment per year in the project. As with payback, management determines a minimal acceptable return to use as a criterion for accepting project proposals.

For many of the capital expenditures proposed by product managers, these two models will be sufficient. The advantage of both is their simplicity. However, both ignore the timing of the cash flows. For riskier or more expensive projects, and those requiring longer time periods to recoup the investment, capital budgeting models that incorporate the time value of money may be preferred. Most analysts use some kind of discounted cash flow analysis to evaluate projects. The key point is that a specific amount of money in the future is worth less than it is today. Net present value and internal rate of return incorporate the time value of money.

The *net present value* (NPV) of a project, computed at the time of the proposal, is the present value of the difference between the total of the years of net revenue and the initial investment. If the future cash inflows, expressed in today's dollars, are greater than the investment (i.e., if the net present value is greater than zero), the project is profitable. However, this method does not indicate what rate of return the project is earning—useful information for comparing projects.

When comparing different projects, the present value index (a modification of the net present value) might be used. The *present value index (PVI)* is the ratio of the present value of cash inflows and the present value of the investment as shown here.

$$PVI = \frac{\text{Present value of cash inflows}}{\text{Present value of the investment}}$$

Let's assume an example of a firm evaluating two separate project proposals from a product manager. The present value of the future revenue for Project A is $60,000 and for B is $35,000. The initial investment is $40,000 and $20,000, respectively. The net present value and present value index of each is shown in the following table:

	PRESENT VALUE OF FUTURE REVENUES (A)	INITIAL INVESTMENT (B)	NET PRESENT VALUE (A – B)	PRESENT VALUE INDEX (A ÷ B)
Project A	$60,000	$40,000	$20,000	1.50
Project B	$35,000	$20,000	$15,000	1.75

In this example, even though Project A is expected to have a higher net present value, Project B may provide a more efficient use of the firm's assets (all else being equal).

As mentioned earlier, the NPV method does not indicate what rate of return a project is earning. The *internal rate of return* (IRR) is the discount rate that equates the present value of future returns with the present value of the investment. (In other words, it is the rate that makes the net present value equal to zero.) The resulting IRR percentage is an interest rate that can be compared to a firm's cost of money or a return required for a certain risk class of investment. Since there is a potential opportunity cost involved in any investment, it's important to know that the return on the investment is acceptable. A riskier project may be expected to generate a higher rate of return than a less risky project. Obviously, the rates should exceed the so-called "risk-free" rates that companies could get by simply putting the money into the bank, or the opportunity costs—those returns that could be earned from alternative investments.

Regardless of the method used to evaluate capital investment projects, it's important that the product manager does not expect the model to make the decision. The calculations are simply data inputs into a decision that should incorporate a variety of other variables. Remember that the calculations are based on a number of estimates, such as (but not limited to):

- initial investment
- direct project costs
- estimated demand converted into a sales forecast
- actual selling price
- timing of cash flows
- product lifecycle

Each of these estimates is subject to prediction error, which should be taken into account in the analysis. Additionally, qualitative factors such as competitive positioning, brand equity protection, and long-term stability should be part of the evaluation.

Step Six: Ascertain Your Firm's Criteria for Evaluating Capital Expenditures

Based on your completion of Step Five, you should understand the probability and riskiness of outcomes for capital investment projects. What hurdle rates are used by your firm to approve projects with that level of riskiness? Have you incorporated qualitative factors that balance or redefine the importance of these hurdles?

KEY POINTS

- Work with your finance department to clarify the fixed and variable costs associated with your products.
- Establish standards to use to develop a flexible product budget.
- Experiment with different sales statistics to determine the most useful tool for decision making.
- Use cost data as a decision tool, but not as the sole criterion in decision making.
- Evaluate the biggest expense categories in descending order to look for areas to improve cost-effectiveness.
- Don't limit your analysis of costs to historical data. Also look at their relevance for future decisions.
- Become familiar with your company's hurdle rates for evaluating capital projects.
- Don't expect a financial analysis to make a decision for you.

6

Product and Brand Portfolio Analysis

"Don't be afraid to fail. You've failed many times, although you may not remember. You fell down the first time you tried to walk. You almost drowned the first time you tried to swim, didn't you? Did you hit the ball the first time you swung a bat? Heavy hitters, the ones who hit the most home runs, also strike out a lot. R. H. Macy failed seven times before his store in New York caught on. English novelist John Creasy got 753 rejection slips before he published 564 books. Babe Ruth struck out 1,330 times, but he also hit 714 home runs. Don't worry about failure. Worry about chances you miss when you don't even try."

—United Technologies Corporation

Companies generally evaluate product portfolios on the basis of *new-product* metrics, most of which (profitability, risk reduction, and strategic initiatives) are internal. While these concepts are absolutely critical, portfolio analysis should go one step further and explore how products across the full range of their lifecycles meld together to provide customer solutions. Keep looking for new ways to use your product line to satisfy customer needs. Does the hospital want a new product that is a complete operating room system, or does it want new products that integrate with equipment already in place? Does the business complex want a totally new information system, or does it want new products that interface with existing hardware and software? Does the contractor want an isolated HVAC system or an indoor environment system that includes a variety of other utilities? By looking at a product mix from the perspective of customer solutions and comparing it to what already exists internally, a company develops a more customer-focused approach to portfolio management that incorporates both new and old

FIGURE 6.1 *Types of Product Line Focus*

products. Four concepts will be discussed in this chapter: (1) product line planning; (2) brand equity management; (3) global product planning; and (4) product rationalization.

Product Line Planning

To develop a plan for your product line, start with strategic goals (see Chapter 7) and business objectives (see Chapter 3), as well as a thorough understanding of target customers. Your strategy can be to develop products only for a particular product-market niche (niche focus), to develop variations of a given product for several markets (product focus), or to develop a complete line of products for a given market segment (market focus), as shown in Figure 6.1. Baking soda, for example, started as a niche product, then grew into various applications across market segments (product focus). It was used as a cat litter ingredient, refrigerator deodorizer, and toothpaste. On the other hand, product managers in service industries like banking and healthcare generally focus a group of offerings on the needs of select market segments such as the small business market or the women's market (market focus).

Product line planning requires deciding on issues such as how many products to have in a line, how to position each product, what comprises the total product in the minds of the customers, how to improve the value proposition of a product, and a host of other factors. While there are no pat answers to any of these questions, they are aspects a product manager should consider.

The number of products for which a given product manager is responsible can vary from one to thousands. Several factors are relevant to the actual number. What is the financial risk and significance of the products? The higher the revenue

FIGURE 6.2 *Benefits of the Tangible Product*

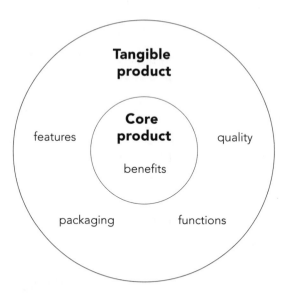

and value to the company, the fewer products a line is likely to have. What is the ratio of new and existing products? The more emphasis on new products, the more likely there will be less time to devote to an extensive product line. How different are the products in terms of manufacture, marketing, and/or customer contact? The more diverse the products are in terms of support needs, the smaller the number of products a given person can handle individually. What specific tasks does the company expect of product managers? A varied or in-depth set of tasks will limit the number of different offerings a product manager can handle. A careful examination of both efficiency and effectiveness is necessary to match product line breadth and depth with an assessment of corporate, competitive, and customer changes.

Product managers should have a thorough understanding of the competitive positioning of products in their line. Positioning refers to how customers perceive your offering compared to that of your competitors. In some situations, the differentiation is based on the product itself. In that case the core product consists of the benefits a customer gets from the tangible product, as shown in Figure 6.2. A core benefit of a high-quality product might be safety. A core benefit of more advanced functions might be ease of use. In cases like this, competitive differentiation can result from distinct product features and attributes.

FIGURE 6.3 *Benefits of the Tangible Product*

But for many, if not most, products the differentiation goes beyond the actual product to include ancillary services, company image, and complementary products. The more similar the tangible product is to the competition, the more important the total solution variables become in terms of both getting and keeping the customers. Therefore, the true benefits a customer derives from buying from you go well beyond the product, as shown in Figure 6.3. Product managers must consider what the customers are *buying* rather than what they themselves are *selling*. In fact, when products are virtually identical, the differentiation that customers are buying results from the core benefits of the *total solution product*, rather than the core benefits of the tangible product.

FIGURE 6.4 *Evaluating Product Differentiators*

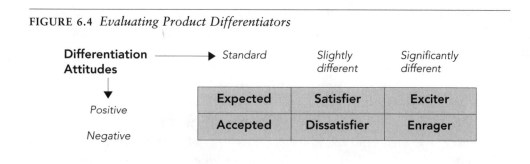

The preceding discussion implies that product managers must manage on two levels: the tangible product level and the total solutions level. What changes (if any) would make the tangible product more profitable? What changes beyond the product can increase the value proposition for customers?

Think about the tangible attributes of the product. Which are viewed positively by customers? Which are viewed negatively? Are there any attributes that cost you money to provide but are nonissues to customers? How have the customer perceptions changed over time? Some of the attributes are standard to a product category, some are slightly different from the competition, and some are significantly different from the competition, as shown in Figure 6.4.[1]

When you have a positive attribute that performs significantly better than the competition, or that no other competitor offers, this attribute may be an exciter that would prompt customers to choose your product. For example, when cars first began offering air conditioning, it was a novel feature desired by customers. As more companies added air conditioning, it was no longer an exciter, but could still be a differentiator (i.e., satisfier) if it performed better than the competition. As the feature became standard, customers began to expect it. So for positive attributes (top row of Figure 6.4), the competitive evolution is from right to left. On the other hand, some attributes are disliked by the customers. If they are standard to an industry (for example, the length of time it takes to boot up a computer), customers may tolerate them until something better comes along. Once competitors eliminate or improve on the attribute, products that retain the attribute become increasingly unacceptable to customers. Customer reaction to

---

1. Adapted from Ian C. MacMillan and Rita Gunther McGrath, "Discover Your Products' Hidden Potential," *Harvard Business Review*, May-June 1996, pp. 58+. The article provides a more in-depth discussion of positive, negative, and neutral product attributes and their impact on the decisions a product manager may need to make.

Reflection Point

How can I improve the value proposition of my product line?

- What new *exciters* can I add to the product?
- What *enragers* can I eliminate?

- What different *versions* of my product and total solution would increase the value to my customers?
- What can I do to make the differences visible and important to customers?

the attribute moves from being grudgingly accepted, to being a dissatisfier, to eventually being an enrager. For negative attributes (bottom row), the evolution over time is from left to right.

The message for product managers is that the acceptance or rejection of specific features and attributes is a constantly moving target. What is an exciter today may eventually become an expected feature—and it is necessary to continually search for that next exciter. Similarly, negative attributes that are accepted by customers today might eventually turn into enragers that cause customers to shift to the competition in droves. Consequently, it is necessary to seek improvements to negative aspects of your product and to do so at a faster pace than the competition.

Product strategy should also look into the need set of different market segments to determine whether different offerings could be used to address certain customer needs. The different offerings could be the result of *product versioning* (the creation of different product variations to appeal to the needs of different market segments) or *solution versioning* (the creation of different solutions beyond the actual product). Different product versions can result from modifying the color, size, texture, intensity, fragrance, taste, sound, or other aspect of various attributes. These versions may better fit a particular market's need without requiring a change in the supporting services, price, or sales process.

On the other hand, some products can be sold virtually "as is," but tailored to a specific market's needs by changing some ancillary service(s) or bundling them with different products to provide a better overall solution to specific customers. For example, two companies may purchase the same computer, one as a do-it-yourself project and the other with supporting installation and repair services. The different solutions fit the customer needs in different ways, even though the tangible products are identical.[2]

Brand Equity Management

Part of product line planning is assuring that the brand equity of all products in your line (including any of the different versions mentioned earlier) work both together and with the corporate brand. Product managers must determine whether a brand image can be stretched across the entire line or whether different brand names are preferred. Also, for most services and for business-to-business products, the product brand identity is directly linked to the corporate brand identity. For example, companies such as Boeing, Electronic Data Systems (EDS), Xerox, IBM, and General Electric place a heavy emphasis on the corporate brand, and any product brands that exist fall under the corporate "halo."

Take a look at the brand architecture in Figure 6.5. The corporate brand may be an "endorser" brand—and sometimes the only brand of value to customers. What do customers perceive the identity of the company to be? What are the rational components of the brand? What are the emotional components? Are these important to the customer? Do they differentiate the firm from the competition? Even though product managers may not have any control over the corporate brand identity, they must be aware of its impact on product sales.

Beyond the corporate brand, there may be business units and/or divisions, product lines (or families), or individual products that have their own brand identities. Different brands may be used at these various levels for a variety of purposes.[3] One reason to use a different brand may be to reach a new market without changing existing brand identity. For example, General Mills is appealing to the growing organic market with a cereal brand called Cascadian Farm.[4] Another reason for bringing out a new brand is to provide a low-end entry

2. See Chapter 8 of Linda Gorchels, *The Product Manager's Handbook* (Chicago: NTC Business Books, 2000) for tips on brainstorming product attributes to add value.

3. See Kevin Lane Keller, *Strategic Brand Management* (New York: Prentice Hall, 1998) for a good discussion of brand management techniques.

4. Kevin Helliker, "In Natural Foods, A Big Name's No Big Help," *The Wall Street Journal*, June 7, 2002, p. B1.

FIGURE 6.5 *Brand Architecture*

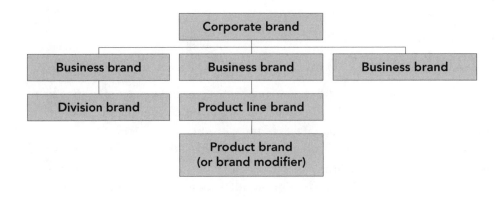

FIGURE 6.6 *Brand Development Template*

Profile target customers.	Portray customers in both objective and subjective terms.
Define differentiation.	Explain how you are different from the competition and why customers care.
Define brand personality.	List the rational and emotional components of your brand.
Determine what customers believe you have promised.	Describe what customers expect in terms of product and service performance, business support, quality, trustworthiness, etc.
Translate promises into standards of performance.	Detail the training, support, and performance measures and define responsibility and authority.
Evaluate depth and scope.	Discuss brand architecture linking corporate issues with brand issues.

Reflection Point

What is the brand image of the products in my line?

- What attributes would customers use to describe each of my products or my company?

- How differentiated is my product's image from the competition's—and do the customers care?

- What attributes are common across all of my products?

product. Intel, for example, named its low-end chip platform Celeron™ rather than Pentium™ to reach a price-sensitive market without reducing the price point of its flagship brand. On the other hand, companies may choose a different brand name for a higher-end prestige offering. Black & Decker chose DeWalt (a product line brand) for its professional products. In the automotive industry, different brand identities are often used for business units offering a more prestigious product line; Toyota chose Lexus, and Honda selected Acura.

Product managers must be able to effectively communicate the positioning of the brand(s). (This will be discussed in Chapter 11.) The brand development template in Figure 6.6 provides the framework for future brand communications and helps you identify what performance measures and training are necessary to sustain a *deliverable* brand promise.

Global Product Planning

In the past decades, product management has evolved dramatically. Increased focus on globalization adds customer management, value chain analysis, global product development, and customer development to the product manager's job description. These new responsibilities require new and different approaches. Here are a few tips for global product planning.

1. **Start with global thinking rather than global sales.** Many product managers don't begin to think globally until after they have received that first inquiry from a distributor or customer from another country. The planning should start long before that. Take a look at your competitors, your

suppliers, and your current customers. Are any of them global? Do your global competitors sell to the same customers as you do? If so, study their foreign (or global) strategies to anticipate possible tactics with your domestic customers. If you have foreign suppliers, evaluate their pricing and marketing approach in other countries to improve your supply chain operations. If your customers have global operations, determine what modifications you might make in your product offering to increase your account penetration.

2. **Embed both domestic and international standards into products and services.** Meeting the UL standards may be appropriate for U.S. markets, but those standards may not be sufficient to meet the requirements in other countries. If your products can be designed up front to meet both domestic and international standards, the potential market for future sales is expanded greatly—without the need for retrofitting a domestic product.

3. **Standardize the core product.** Even though there's an obvious benefit to designing products to meet a variety of standards, the idea of a fully standardized global product that is identical all over the world is a near myth. Some of the benefits of global products (or services), however, can be achieved by standardizing the core product, or large parts of it, while customizing peripheral or other parts of the product. In passenger automobiles, for example, product standardization comes primarily in the platform (the chassis and related parts) and, to a lesser extent, the engine. The auto industry has been talking about global cars for decades, but implementation has been difficult at best. Honda made progress with its 1998 Accord. By coming up with a platform that can be bent and stretched into markedly different vehicles, Honda saved hundreds of millions of dollars in development costs. By moving the car's gas tank back between the rear tires, Honda engineers discovered they could design a series of special brackets that would allow them to hook the wheels to the car's more flexible inner subframe. Rather than shipping the same car around the globe, only the underlying platform was used worldwide.

4. **Identify the appropriate level of adaptation required.** Regardless of the attempt to standardize products or product lines globally, various levels of adaptation will be required. Some products need only different language

Reflection Point

Have I considered global opportunities for my products or services?

• Are my competitors, customers, or suppliers global? What impact does that have on my products?

• If I am selling in other countries, do I need to adapt the product each time? What improvements can I make to the adaptation process?

• What parts of the product or service can I standardize as a "core"?

documentation. For example, when Minolta cameras were shipped in the 1990s from Japan to New Wave Enterprise (a distribution center at the Port of Antwerp in Belgium), they were shipped without support materials. Language-specific (e.g., French, Dutch, German, etc.) documentation was added when the products were shipped across land to other destinations in Europe.

Other products could have their lifecycles extended by looking for the best fit between local market needs and product capabilities. For example, the current U.S. technology for anesthesia ventilators allows plus or minus a few milliliters of oxygen accuracy. However, many Latin American operating rooms are satisfied with plus or minus *100* milliliters of accuracy, with a commensurately lower price. A major supplier of anesthesia equipment found it could prolong the life of its "unsophisticated" ventilators by offering them in these markets at a much lower price than the state-of-the-art equipment.

This reasoning can apply to consumer products as well. Take basic flour as an example. India consumes about 69 million tons of wheat a year (compared to 26 million tons in the United States), yet almost no whole-wheat flour is sold prepackaged. Selling packaged flour in India is almost revolutionary; most Indian housewives still buy raw wheat in bulk, clean it by hand, and, on a weekly basis, carry some to a neighborhood mill, or *chakki*, where it is ground between two stones. Pillsbury found it could increase the sales of basic prepackaged flour (a mature product in the United States) by appealing to this market, and it has modified the Pillsbury Doughboy to pitch this "old" product as something new in India.

Reflection Point

Do I have any *cockroach* products in my line?

- What process exists for evaluating products for elimination? What criteria are (or should be) used?

- What would be the impact on my product line and on the company if select products were eliminated?

- What strategies are appropriate for eliminating the identified products?

5. **Anticipate global competition.** With increasing competition able to react quickly when new products are introduced, worldwide planning at the product level provides a number of tangible benefits. First, product managers will be better able to develop products with specifications compatible on a global scale. Second, they will be able to more effectively and efficiently adapt products to local needs. And finally, they will be able to respond more quickly to competitive moves of global companies.

Product Rationalization

Most companies have some standardization in their new product development processes, but fewer are consistent in their processes to eliminate products ("rationalize" product lines). Certain products consequently become so difficult to get rid of that some firms refer to them as *cockroach* products. Developing a list of criteria to use to evaluate products can be in everyone's best interest. Unnecessary products consume financial and physical resources that can better be used in other ways. Here are some criteria to consider in product rationalization:

- sales volume, revenue, profitability
- percentage part commonality
- impact of elimination on overall product line
- ability to combine functionality of various products
- customer need or competitive advantage
- potential shift of allocated overhead to other products

Once a product has been identified as a candidate for elimination, the best way to accomplish that task must still be decided. Should the price be raised so that customers decide on their own to discontinue buying it (and hopefully switch to another of your products)? Should the price be lowered to reduce inventory? Should the rights be sold to another company?

KEY POINTS

- Start your product line planning with strategic goals and specific business objectives.
- Think beyond the features of your product in identifying benefits desired by your customers. Include benefits of both the product and the extended solution.
- Carefully manage the equity of both your corporate and product brands.
- Consider offering different product versions with different brand names to appeal to different market segments.
- If appropriate, evaluate global opportunities for your product.
- Establish a systematic process (with clear and relevant criteria) for product rationalization.

PRODUCT PORTFOLIO CHECKLIST

PRODUCT LINE PLANNING

Is the breadth and depth of your product line manageable?	Yes	No
Have you identified potential changes to your tangible product?	Yes	No
Have you identified potential changes to your total solution?	Yes	No
Do you have new exciters in the pipeline?	Yes	No
Do you apply product or solution versioning to best meet the needs of differentiated market segments?	Yes	No

BRAND EQUITY MANAGEMENT

Does your existing brand have a unique, differentiated, positive identity with customers?	Yes	No
Does the product brand benefit from a corporate halo?	Yes	No

PRODUCT PORTFOLIO CHECKLIST, *continued*

Can you stretch the product brand?	Yes	No
Would your line benefit from the addition of new brands?	Yes	No
Have you completed the brand development template?	Yes	No

GLOBAL PRODUCT PLANNING

Have you considered global opportunities for your products or services?	Yes	No
Are your competitors, customers, or suppliers global?	Yes	No
Have you incorporated this information into your plans?	Yes	No
Can you adapt your product to fit in other countries?	Yes	No
Can you develop a standard core product that will require less adaptation?	Yes	No

PRODUCT RATIONALIZATION

Do you have any *cockroach* products in your line?	Yes	No
Do you have a process to evaluate them for elimination?	Yes	No
Are the criteria clear, relevant, and appropriate?	Yes	No
Before you decide to drop a product, do you carefully consider the impact it may have on other products in your line?	Yes	No
Before you decide to drop a product, do you develop a strategy for the process?	Yes	No

7

Strategic Visioning and Planning

"If we could predict the future with certainty, it would mean that the future could not be changed. . . . Yet this is the main purpose of studying the future: to look at what may happen if present trends continue, decide if this is what is desirable, and if it's not, work to change it. . . . The ability to see and create the future is the essence of leadership."

—World Future Society

Strategic visioning is a technique sometimes believed to be used only by the corporate part of management. It's not. Product managers must develop visions and plans for their product lines to be successful in the future. Strategy is the art and science of attaining sustainable competitive advantage through the most appropriate utilization of resources and assets. It starts with the environmental scan (as discussed in Chapter 3) and then requires leadership in defining the product line's future direction, making trade-offs, and structuring an implementation plan.

Strategic Thinking

Let's do some visioning for your product. Think about what you would like your product line to look like in the future. Pick a date five or so years into the future and assume it is that date. Now, write an annual report for your product line. What products would you be selling? At what stage of the product lifecycle will

FIGURE 7.1 *Product Management Goal Alignment*

they be, and what will that mean in terms of strategy? Who would your strategic customers be? What would their brand perception of you be? How large would your line be in units, revenue, and profitability? And, of course, don't forget to think about the "total solution" product that differentiates you from the competition. As Tony Manning states in his book *Making Sense of Strategy*, "strategy must enable your organization to make a difference that matters to a critical mass of the 'right' customers."[1] So, for your product line, what *really matters*? What really matters to your customers? What really matters to your company?

Many product managers make the mistake of projecting the past forward and using that as their view of the future. While the past is an important aspect of planning, product managers should also think about the external trends and changes that could impact their offerings. What is your firm's growth strategy

---

1. Tony Manning, *Making Sense of Strategy* (New York: AMACOM, 2002) preface.

FIGURE 7.2 *Strategy Requires Thinking and Planning*

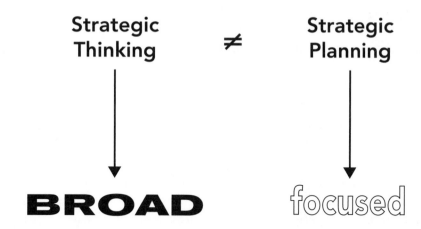

(i.e., what really matters to your firm vis-à-vis your product line)? Will it be positioned the same in the future as it is now, or is it moving in a different direction? What impact might that have on your product line? From a strategic perspective, product managers must determine whether they are being effective—doing the right things. From a tactical and operational perspective, they must determine whether they are doing things right—accomplishing the stated goals. For example, who have you identified as the strategic customers you want to align with (a strategic goal)? How well are you retaining these customers when you get them (as a consequence of your tactical plans)? What are you and others in your firm doing on an ongoing basis to retain these customers (i.e., your operational activities)? The relationship among these is shown in Figure 7.1.

The relationship among strategies, tactics, and operational activities implies that this is an ongoing process rather than a once-a-year activity. Product managers should be continually engaged in strategic *thinking*, even though the strategic *planning* activities may be less frequent (see Figure 7.2). Strategic thinking is very broad, requiring product managers to look at all market shifts and new competitors. But you can't chase all of the opportunities or problems implied by these potential futures. You have to decide on a particular direction and plan a strategy for it alone. And planning a strategy for one direction means that you are *not* going in a different direction. This strategic planning is narrower than strategic thinking, requiring product managers to "put a stake in the ground" and prepare to spend time and money moving in a stated direction.

Strategic thinking requires a broad look at both customers and competitors. Think about customers and their needs in the future as well as their needs of today. Answer the following questions:

- How will customers of tomorrow be different from customers of today? How will that affect how you do business?
- What products will these customers expect or demand?
- Will you need to develop new products or markets?
- Do your existing resources, assets, and capabilities provide a competitive advantage today? Will they tomorrow?

Since customers are buying solutions to problems (instead of just products), it's important to look at the competition in that context. In the near-term, which competitors most directly solve the problems customers have? These would be the most direct competitors—those that you have lost business to or gained business from. In the long-term, people may use completely different products to provide the same benefits or "functionalities." For example, a person buying a compact car may consider the Honda Accord, Toyota Corolla, or Saturn as competitors. A more broadly defined set of competitors may include anything from a VW bug to a BMW. Still more broadly defined competitors that address the need of transportation might include motorbikes, trucks, and vans. Looking still more broadly, competition might include public transportation, or even a vacation that uses the budget that was earmarked for the car. Think about your competitors along this continuum and complete the following information:

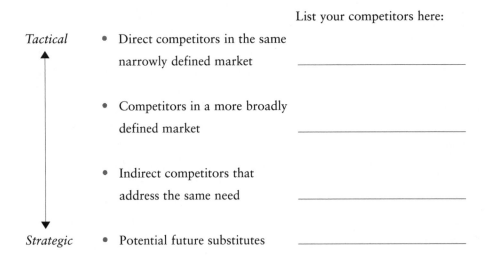

List your competitors here:

Tactical

- Direct competitors in the same narrowly defined market
  _____

- Competitors in a more broadly defined market
  _____

- Indirect competitors that address the same need
  _____

Strategic

- Potential future substitutes
  _____

Reflection Point

What is the vision for my product line?

- What customers, products, and brand perceptions provide the future for my product area?

- What emerging business models (or competitors) might cause customers to migrate away from my offerings?

- What really matters to my customers and my company?

Product managers are both managers and leaders. As managers they must execute plans in an increasingly complex world. As leaders they must deal with ongoing change. John Kotter, Professor of Leadership at Harvard, has written extensively about the differences between management and leadership.

Leadership and management are two distinctive and complementary systems of action. Management is about coping with complexity. Leadership is about coping with change. Leadership complements management; it doesn't replace it. Companies manage complexity by planning and budgeting, by controlling and problem solving. By contrast, leading an organization begins by setting direction, aligning people to the direction, and inspiring people to achieve a vision.

—JOHN P. KOTTER

Good strategists are good change agents. Product managers will continue to face change at an accelerated pace in the future. How well they adapt will be a key to their survival. As Alvin Toffler noted in *Future Shock*, "fact" and "fiction" change with time, and "even the most highly skilled and intelligent members of society" will have difficulty keeping up with the information explosion.

Strategy Development

A primary goal for strategy formulation is to establish competitive advantage through the development and deployment of resources, assets, and capabilities. Think about where you are now (the environmental scan) and where you want

FIGURE 7.3 *Strategy Requires Trade-Offs and Balance*

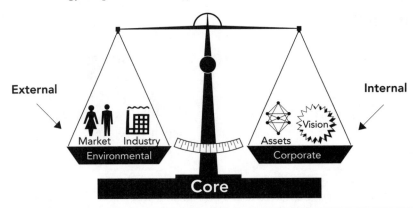

to go (your strategic vision). Closing the gap between where you are and where you want to go will require effective use of your resources, assets, and capabilities and may occasionally require modifying your vision. In other words, you may need to make trade-offs between your vision and your internal capabilities to balance them against the external realities of your customers (market) and competitors (industry). The fulcrum of this balance is your "core business," as shown in Figure 7.3.

You can develop a strategy for your product line in a number of ways. You can optimize your core business by adding to your product line or customer base. You can look for ways to more fully utilize the assets at your disposal. Or you can attempt to capitalize on industry or marketplace trends. Each of these approaches to strategy development will be discussed in this section.

Optimize Core Business

Your *core business* refers to those products, customers, and technologies that are your ongoing source of competitive advantage. Ask yourself the following questions:

If you ceased to offer your product line, what loss would your customers experience?

- How easily could they get their needs satisfied elsewhere?
- Which customers would be most affected (i.e., who are your core customers)?

What is the source of your competitive advantage?

- Customer relationships?
- Cost?
- Product features and performance?
- Services?
- Brand equity?
- Streamlined processes?

Is your advantage difficult for competitors to imitate? Is it durable over time? Can customers find substitutes for it?

Answering these questions helps you identify your core business.[2] Once you have done that, you must decide the best way to extend this core to new opportunities. Let's say that you are a product manager for electric typewriters. Your core business could be providing communication and information capabilities to businesses, or your core business could be providing electromechanical products to consumers through retail channels. Even though the product is the same, the means of growing from the core are different. IBM was in the first situation and was able to move from typewriters to PCs due to its competences in mainframes and sales channels. Remington, on the other hand, moved from typewriters to electric shavers. Both attempted to build on the strength of their core business. As you explore various strategies to extend your core business, keep in mind that you are trying to move from where you are today to where you want to be in the future (i.e., your vision), and the selected strategy should focus on that direction.

Leverage Assets and Resources

Strategy development can also emerge from examining your assets and resources and looking for ways to optimize how they are used. Resources may be financial (available funds for investment), physical (a factory or location), technological (patents), reputational (brand equity), or human (skill sets). If you have a financial resource, you may be able to optimize it by using it to acquire a complementary product line, or by offering low or no finance charges to stimulate sales. Physical resources might be optimized by finding additional uses for them. For

---

2. For more detail on defining and expanding your core business, refer to Chris Zook, *Profit from the Core* (Boston: Harvard Business School Press, 2001).

example, fast-food restaurants try to encourage customers to frequent them for breakfast and dinner (as well as lunch) to be able to attain a more consistent utilization rate of the building and related resources. Technological resources, such as intellectual assets and properties, might be enhanced by licensing them to obtain patent royalties. Reputational assets might be leveraged by extending a brand from an existing product into new product categories. Human assets might be optimized by having a common brand focus. Think about ways you might be able to leverage your firm's assets and resources strategically.

ASSETS AND RESOURCES	IDEAS TO LEVERAGE
Financial	_____
Physical	_____
Technological	_____
Reputational	_____
Human	_____

As was stated in the discussion on growing your core business, this approach could yield several different growth strategies. To select those that are most relevant, focus on closing the gap between where you are and where you want to go.

Respond to Trends

Your environmental scan may have identified some positive trends that could be capitalized on, or some negative trends that may need to be overcome. Examine the following trends (from A to Z) and indicate what impacts if any they might have on your planning. Substitute industry-specific trends, if necessary.

TREND	POTENTIAL IMPLICATIONS FOR YOUR BUSINESS
Aging population	_____
Biomedical and drug advances	_____
Crisis of trust in leaders	_____
Digital explosion	_____

Education shifts _____

Fluctuating economy _____

Globalization _____

Healthcare changes _____

Information overload _____

Job redefinition _____

Knowledge management _____

Lifelong learning _____

Mergers _____

New sales channels _____

Obesity anxiety _____

Privacy concerns _____

Quality _____

Robotics _____

Sustainability _____

Technology _____

Uncertainty _____

Virtual reality _____

Workforce productivity _____

Xtreme sports _____

You, Inc. _____

Zoom-zoom (speed) _____

FIGURE 7.4 *Customer Value Chain*

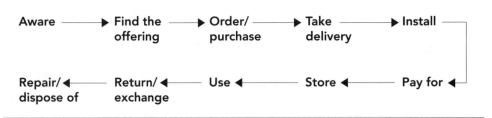

Another way of looking at trends is through the eyes of your customers. What opportunities exist to differentiate your offerings throughout the customer value chain—from first becoming aware of the product, to buying and using it, to eventually disposing of it? (See the customer value chain in Figure 7.4.)

How do customers first become aware of their need for your product, and what can you do to influence it? The Oral B toothbrush, for example, has a blue stripe that wears out with usage to indicate when it is time for the customer to buy a new toothbrush. In this case, the "trigger" to buy a new product is built into the design of the product. Sometimes awareness comes from the communications and packaging. Baking soda packaged with vents for use in a refrigerator increases the awareness of using the product in that manner.

Some companies have an advantage when their product is easier to find than the competition. McDonald's golden arches provide a recognizable symbol that helps customers quickly find the restaurant. Appropriate domain names help people find information about a company on the Internet.

Simplifying the ordering process may provide a benefit to a specific segment of customers. With the growth of the Internet, 24/7 has increasingly become an expectation. But many customers still long for the personal contact and advice that is not possible electronically.

Making it easy for customers to take delivery of a product can also be beneficial. Furniture delivery, cable TV installation, and similar services are increasingly being offered in the evening or on weekends rather than requiring customers to take time off from work in order to be home at a designated time.

Simplifying installation can be another benefit to customers. When PC companies began color-coding the cables that connect the monitor, CPU, keyboard, and other apparatus, it took some of the guesswork out of the process.

Simplifying the payment process may provide a benefit to a specific segment of customers. Busy customers have appreciated gas stations that provide credit card payment at the pump, or bar code scanning of their cars at tollbooths.

Reflection Point

What strategies are going to be necessary to reach the goals stated in my product line vision?

- How can I extend my core business?

- What assets or resources can I leverage, and how can I optimize them?
- What trends can I capitalize on (or reduce the negative impact of)?

Many credit card companies offer an automatic debit program where the amount in the monthly bill is automatically transferred from the customer's checking account to the credit card company.

Making it easier to store your product may provide some advantages. Coca-Cola recently introduced its "fridge pack" that is designed to fit easily in a refrigerator, with an opening in front to dispense the cans. Some insurance companies have found that customers appreciate having their policies stored electronically to simplify understanding coverage and filing claims.

Helping customers use a product or service to their greatest benefit can be another advantage. The use of telephone hotlines, FAQs, and customer-friendly instruction manuals can help with relationship building.

Although returns and exchanges need to be monitored carefully by companies, their importance to customers cannot be minimized. Companies that provide reasonable policies can gain the loyalty of customers who have experienced unreasonable policies.

The last aspect of the customer value chain involves the repair or disposal of a product. Although not relevant to all products, it can be an issue for objects such as appliances, batteries, motor oil, and other items with potentially hazardous materials. Companies that simplify the process for their customers may find a potential competitive advantage over those who don't.

Strategy Implementation

For product managers to be change agents, they must be able to implement strategies. And they must be able to implement them through other individuals. There are several things that must exist for this type of implementation to be effective. First, people must agree that the change is necessary. There must be a belief that the status quo is not acceptable, that the business opportunity addressed in the strategy is real, attainable, and consistent with the firm's strategy, and that the gain of pursuing it outweighs the pain.

Next, product managers must overcome barriers to change and implementation of the strategy. What turf barriers, personality issues, and differing goals stand in the way of successful implementation? As you develop the strategic plan for your product, think about the factors that might impede implementation and think of ways to minimize the negative impact of those factors.

FACTORS THAT MAY IMPEDE STRATEGY	WAYS TO MINIMIZE THE NEGATIVE IMPACT

Third, people must understand the *personal* or *individual* implications of the strategy:

- How is this change relevant to what I do?
- What, specifically, should I do?
- How will I be measured and what consequences will I face?
- What's in it for me?

And finally, there should be a system of strategic feedback and learning so that the strategy is not static. The feedback should include (a) whether the strategy is being executed, and (b) if the assumptions underlying the strategy are still viable.

KEY POINTS
- Look for strategies that make a difference to your customers, your company, and your product line.

Reflection Point

How effectively do I communicate the vision for my products to other people in the company?

- Do others agree with the importance of the strategy for the company?

- Is there a personal understanding of, and commitment to, the strategy?
- How well do I communicate a sense of urgency for the strategic direction?

- Develop a future annual report for your product to help you envision the future.
- Conduct both strategic thinking and strategic planning activities.
- Identify future customer profiles, needs, and changes.
- Identify future competitor strategies (both direct and indirect).
- Clarify and optimize your core business.
- Identify assets and resources you can leverage to grow your product line.
- Identify trends that you can build into your strategic planning.
- Look for opportunities to create advantage throughout the customer value chain.
- Communicate and obtain buy-in to your vision to enable implementation.

STRATEGY CHECKLIST

STRATEGIC THINKING

Have you visualized what your product line will be in the future?　　Yes　　No

Do you avoid simply projecting the past forward?　　Yes　　No

Do you perform both strategic thinking and strategic planning activities?　　Yes　　No

STRATEGY CHECKLIST, *continued*

Have you identified and profiled future customers and their needs?	Yes	No
Have you identified future changes in your competitive arena?	Yes	No
Have you defined what really matters to customers?	Yes	No

STRATEGY DEVELOPMENT

Have you defined the gap between where you are and where you want to go?	Yes	No
Are you aware of the trade-offs you may need to make in developing your strategy?	Yes	No
Can you articulate your core business?	Yes	No
Have you evaluated ways to extend this core to new opportunities?	Yes	No
Have you defined your firm's assets and determined ways to leverage them strategically?	Yes	No
Have you identified trends and built them into your strategies?	Yes	No
Have you looked throughout the customer value chain to identify potential new areas of competitive advantage?	Yes	No

STRATEGY IMPLEMENTATION

Have you convinced others in your organization of the importance of your strategy?	Yes	No
Have you identified factors that may impede the implementation of your strategy?	Yes	No
Did you determine ways to minimize the impact of these factors?	Yes	No
Do others in your firm understand the individual implications of your strategy?	Yes	No
Are they willing to accept these implications?	Yes	No
Have you created a sense of urgency?	Yes	No

Chapter

8

Concept and Development of New Products

"Nothing is more dangerous than an idea when it is the only one you have."

—Emile Chartier, French philosopher
and essayist

Many companies have found that their success in product development comes more from a stream of small wins than from a one-time flood. These successes require a consistent flow of new product ideas that can be evaluated for potential commercialization, ideas that should be part of an overall product strategy, as discussed in Chapter 7. This strategy can be thought of as a funnel (see Figure 8.1) with numerous ideas being input, some being eliminated or screened out as not viable efforts for the company, and ending with successful new products. The more ideas that are evaluated in the process, the greater the likelihood of strong (rather than "good enough") products being the result.

New Product Objectives

A starting point for new product development should be clarifying the objectives the company has for the product line. There may be several objectives that new products are intended to satisfy. Some may be purely financial, while others may relate more directly to specific strategy initiatives. Some examples of strategic new product objectives include the following:

FIGURE 8.1 *The New Product Funnel*

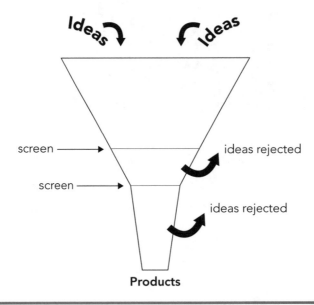

Products

- Provide an inroad to a new market (e.g., a different industrial segment, a growing consumer niche, or a new country).
- Defend market share against foreign competition.
- Prevent loss of sales to a low-priced competitor.
- Position the company as being a "full-solution" provider.
- Increase plant utilization to full capacity.
- Reduce dependence on an old technology.

New product development involves many functions within a company—typically in the form of a new product project team. Product managers, as team leaders or members, may need to bring the voice of the customer to the entire process, from concept generation to sales forecasting to specification writing to beta testing. The end result of the process is commercialization or launch (to be discussed in Chapter 9). A basic flowchart of the process is shown in Figure 8.2. Note that after completing the activities in each box of the flowchart, the product will be reevaluated to determine whether to continue with the project or to cancel it. These evaluations may be called *screens, hurdles, stage-gates, tolls,* or any other term that recognizes the need to make a decision on progressing to the next step of the process.

FIGURE 8.2 *The New Product Development Flowchart*

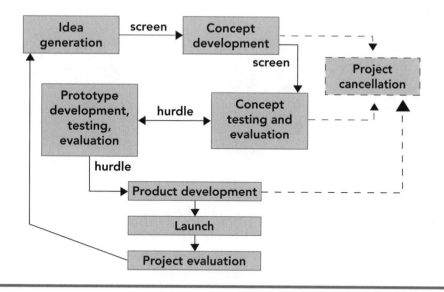

Idea Generation

Product managers who are expected to help a firm achieve its new product objectives must be open to a variety of ideas from numerous sources, both internal and external to the company.[1] Some ideas may result from the strategic thinking activities described in Chapter 7. Others are described here, including customer research techniques, competitive analyses, and various investigative activities.

There are many ways to obtain customer ideas for new products or product changes. Complaint letters, warranty records, and unsolicited requests (sometimes via the sales force) can shed light on customer needs. However, these are reactive techniques. Product managers should also include proactive approaches to gaining customer input. You should devote a solid percentage of your time to talking with your customers (especially the "A" accounts) about their businesses, their goals, and any future needs you might be able to address. Some of these discussions might occur at trade shows and others as part of a program of visits to

---

1. For questions to help you focus on developing product enhancements, refer to Chapters 8 and 9 in Linda Gorchels, *The Product Manager's Handbook* (Chicago: NTC Business Books, 2000).

Reflection Point

How well do I understand the general product (or service) development process in my company?

• What are the overall new product objectives?

• What improvements can I make by linking my product development strategy to the firm's product development objectives?

customer locations. By going to customer locations, it may be possible to get a better understanding of how your product or service is being used and whether there are any adaptations that could be made to improve the usefulness. At least part of the discussion with customers should focus on the outcomes they desire from your product or service—rather than a discussion of new and improved features—since the outcomes might imply a totally different kind of product.[2]

To come up with ideas that are more than "tweaks" of your existing products, determine which of your customers can provide the most insights. Lead users—those who are most likely to have taken the initiative to modify products to meet their requirements—may be the customers you want to contact. These customers are very likely not representative of your overall market; rather, they *lead* the market in a particular direction. In fact, these users may have already "prototyped" the refined product through their adaptations.[3] Sometimes lead users are not even customers. For example, the aerospace industry created innovations such as antilock brakes that were transferable to the automotive industry.

The interviews used to obtain this type of information should consist of open-ended, rather than closed-ended, questions. They should require thoughtful consideration by the customer in answering. Here are some examples:

---

2. The process of gathering and using outcome measures for new product ideation is described in Anthony W. Ulwick, "Turn Customer Input into Innovation," *Harvard Business Review*, January 2002, pp. 91–97.

3. For a more thorough discussion on using lead users to help generate breakthrough ideas, refer to Eric von Hippel, Stefan Thomke, and Mary Sonnack, "Creating Breakthroughs at 3M," *Harvard Business Review*, September–October 1999, pp. 47–57.

- Describe your experiences in using _____.
- What prompted you to buy this type of [product or service] the first time, and what new attributes are you likely to look for in the future?
- Describe the ideal solution to [stated problem]. (Probe beyond product features.)
- What disappoints (or frustrates) you about the existing solutions to this problem?
- Explain in detail how you buy/use/repair/etc. _____.
- Describe the perfect _____, distinguishing between what is absolutely necessary and what would simply be "nice to have."

Note that the responses to these questions and statements yield insights into how to design the product, rather than how many to produce (i.e., the sales forecast).

Analyzing the competition can also shed light on potential product ideas. Take a look at the complete product or service line of your competitors. What are they offering that you don't offer? Is that valuable to your customers? In conducting product-to-product comparisons, are there any features or functionalities that your competitors offer but you don't? Any of these gaps might lead to a new product idea, but be careful to avoid developing a "me-too" product that will not have any competitive advantage.

There are other approaches product managers can use for investigative ideation (i.e., the forming of ideas). See Figure 8.3 for a visual representation of this process. Discussions with R&D may yield discoveries that could be designed into a customer-valued product. Supply chain partners, such as distributors or suppliers, may have ideas to successfully fill out a product line. Market segments with unmet needs could trigger new product ideas. Studying past successes and failures, examining the competencies of other parts of your organization, and using analogies and metaphors can often jump-start the idea generation process.

Your goal in generating new product ideas is to:

- create an ongoing pipeline so that there are products at different stages of development
- help ensure that corporate growth targets can be met
- develop a portfolio with varying degrees of risk

Generally, new ideas are screened throughout development to determine whether or not to continue with the plan. Some screens are intuitive (the

FIGURE 8.3 *Sources of New Product Ideas*

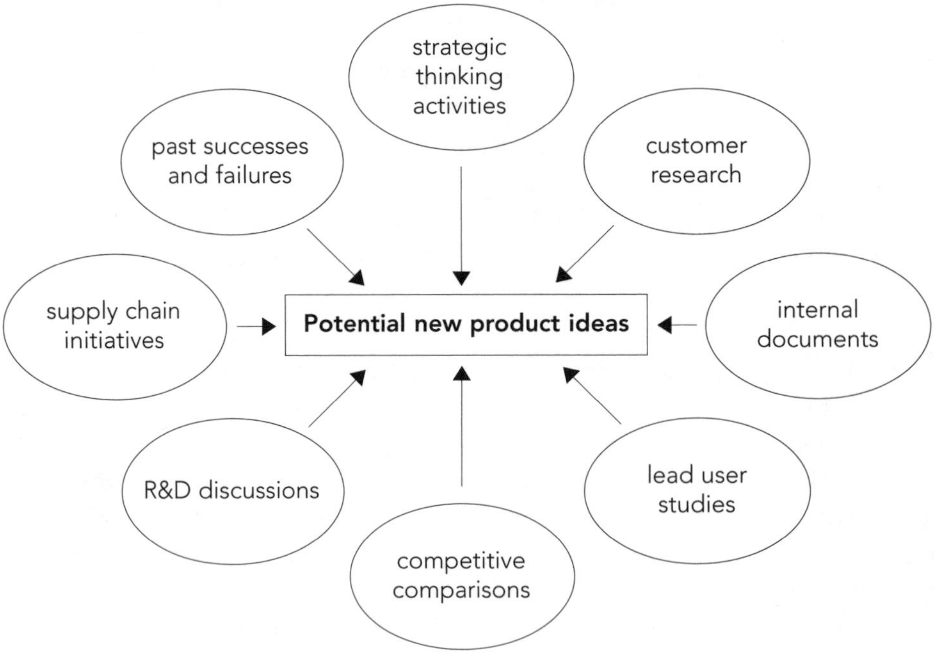

technology required won't be available for at least 25 years!), while others require some basic secondary research. As an idea grows from a concept to a product, it will pass through increasingly more detailed screens.

Forecasting and Concept Screening

Ideas that have passed the preliminary screen (e.g., they are viable and consistent with the firm's strategy) must be further developed and quantified. Product managers must be able to justify their new product idea with a reasonable sales forecast—and when there are several new product ideas being considered by a company, the product manager with the most convincing statistics and sales forecasts generally wins. Sales forecasts represent the product manager's expectations of future sales of the new product.

There is no one right way to forecast, but there are several factors that should be considered in the process. What is the overall market potential for the product and what can you do to obtain a substantial portion of that potential? What

Reflection Point

How effective am I in developing new product ideas?

- How much time do I spend with customers inquiring about future needs?

- What role do lead users play in helping me develop breakthrough ideas?

- How well do I understand the competition in order to maintain an advantage?

buyer and competitor behaviors might restrict or enhance sales? Is this a new-to-the-world product, or are you introducing a new product into a mature market? What is the expected life of the offering compared to similar products?

The research involved in ideation was more qualitative in nature, whereas the research necessary to develop forecasts must combine qualitative and quantitative approaches. It's important to realize that the accuracy of the financial analysis can be no better than the accuracy of the estimated sales.

Forecasts may have several components: market potential, growth rate, customer sales projections, market friction, and company impacts.[4] Market potential is the estimate of sales prospects for any product in the category (yours as well as the competition). Growth rate is the current and projected growth of the category. Much of this type of information is available through secondary sources such as trade association and government statistics. Market potential may be the total number of people in a specific demographic category from census data, or the number of workers in a particular geographic region as compiled from local government and trade sources. Growth rate information for specific types of markets may be expressed as current percentage increases over the past few years, but be careful when projecting that growth rate into the future. Changes in technology, fashion trends, the economy, or other factors could cause the growth rate to either increase or decrease. For estimates of both market potential and growth rate, it may be useful to augment secondary data with input from experts (perhaps internal and external to the company). One

---

4. Refer to Robert J. Thomas, *New Product Development: Managing and Forecasting for Strategic Success* (New York: John Wiley & Sons, 1993), particularly Chapters 7 and 8 for a discussion of new product forecasting considerations and approaches.

approach is the *Delphi method* in which experts are asked for forecasts, along with their rationale for their forecasts. The information is compiled from all the experts then shared with them anonymously. Since each of the experts has access to colleague forecasts and rationale without the peer pressure of face-to-face meetings, the forecasts can be successfully refined in a more objective manner.

Market potential is a good starting point for estimating sales—particularly for completely new products for your company—but the process has to go further. What percent of this potential is reasonable for you to attain? You might be able to estimate this by using your internal market share figures for similar products launched in the past. (An internal Delphi approach might work here as well.) Getting input on each salesperson's territorial sales expectations along with the probability of getting these sales can be another data point in the forecasting process, as long as it is not the only forecasting input. Similarly, input from distributors, agents, and other channel members is worth compiling—especially for line extensions.

Market friction refers to the (primarily external) factors that may inhibit sales. Will the new product require a substantial change in customer behavior? If so, are the advantages of the product sufficient to overcome the resistance to change? Several inventors have unsuccessfully tried to develop an improvement over the Qwerty keyboard. However, since we all learned how to type on this format of keyboard, the improvements were not significant enough to justify behavior change. Can (and will) competitors act swiftly to defeat the new product? Is there any incentive for channel members and other stakeholders to support the new product? Are there any potential technology changes that may hurt (or help) the new product to become successful? The potential impact (in either percentages, unit sales, or dollar amount) should be estimated for the sources of market friction. Although the impact of all these factors are subjective estimates, the process of thinking through them forces a more realistic appraisal of the success chances for the product.

Gathering information from customers on their awareness of the product category (if new), as well as their intentions to purchase your product (or possibly any product in the category) are useful inputs to the forecasting process. For example, if customers are asked their purchase intention on a five-point scale from very likely to very unlikely to buy, the percentage of the "very likely to buy" respondents can be multiplied by your share of market potential to get a general estimate of sales potential. In addition, if the product can be purchased frequently (or if there are consumables connected with the initial purchase), this information can be used to improve the sales estimate.

The final consideration in sales forecasting is the impact of your company actions on the market friction. If the company invests in educating the customer about the value of a new product, lobbies to encourage the government to move in a direction favorable to the new product offering, or hires a specialized sales force, the impact of the market friction may be changed.

Pulling all of these factors together results in a formula for estimating initial sales of a new product:

	market potential *(from secondary and expert sources)*
×	market share *(from your share on similar products)*
×	% likely to buy *(from customer surveys and channel input)*
×	expected volume per purchase *(from customer and channel input)*
× ___	expected number of purchases *(from customer and channel input)*
=	preliminary sales forecast
±	impact of market friction *(internal assessment)*
±	corrective actions taken by company to affect market friction
− ___	any cannibalization of existing products *(internal assessment)*
=	net sales forecast

What's missing from this sales forecast is the trending over time. To determine expected sales over a period of time may require comparing the product to similar products launched in the past and adapting the lifecycle sales to it. The unit sales figures and prices can be combined with expected cost data to develop projected financials. However, it is always worth remembering that each of these data points is an *estimate*, and presenting sales forecasts as concrete is risky at best. Because of the many variables involved in forecasting, product managers may wish to provide estimates of optimistic, pessimistic, and most likely unit sales.

As part of this stage of the product development process, product managers are generally charged with developing a plan or "business case" to help management determine whether additional investment should be made to convert the concept into a product. Basic components of this type of business plan include elements such as:

- executive summary
- relationship of the proposed product to the new product objectives
- general product description
- market analysis (combining both internal/external and primary/secondary data)

- voice of the customer (VOC): user needs and wants
- competition (including strengths/weaknesses and the product's proposed advantages)
- technical assessment (quality function deployment or QFD)
- product development plan (functional involvement, resources, project plan)
- manufacturing plan (capacity requirements)
- launch plan (advertising, sales, pricing, distribution)
- development team (key personnel)
- risk factors (and risk reduction plans)
- financial analysis (expected returns, payback, cash flow, funds needed)
- supporting documents (appendix of research, patents, contracts)

Although bad ideas should be screened out early in the new product development process, it's important that good ideas be left in. This requires having a corporate culture conducive to creativity and innovation. Chic Thompson, in his book, *What a Great Idea!,* talks about the importance of identifying and overcoming "killer phrases" that destroy creativity. He even advocates issuing a "killer phrase arrest warrant" to individuals who consistently restrain original thinking.[5] Examples of killer phrases are shown in Figure 8.4.

That being said, it is nevertheless important to know what criteria are appropriate for screening ideas in an effort to prevent additional investments in bad ideas and to encourage investment in good ideas. Robert Cooper's NewProd™ is an instrument for business executives to use in evaluating proposed new product projects.[6] It contains a series of statements that evaluators use to rate product concepts and has been quite effective in predicting "winners." The statements include factors such as resources required, product complexity, product newness, market size and growth rate, and competitive superiority. Gerald G. Udell has

---

5. Charles "Chic" Thompson, *What a Great Idea!* (New York: HarperPerennial, 1992). This book contains tips and activities for stimulating ideas, jump-starting meetings, and creative approaches to maintaining momentum.

6. NewProd™ is a scoring model developed by Robert G. Cooper that has been revised over time. In his book, *Winning at New Products* (Boston: Addison-Wesley, 1986), the model consisted of 48 statements compiled into five categories: resources required, nature of project, newness of project, the final product, and the market for this product. For each statement (e.g., the market for this product is growing very quickly), individuals evaluate the proposed concept on a scale from 0 to 10, with 0 being "strongly disagree" and 10 being "strongly agree." The evaluators were also asked to indicate how confident they were about their answers. The tool has been updated since that first edition of the book, and NewProd™ is now a commercially available computer-scoring model. Information about it can be obtained at prod-dev.com.

FIGURE 8.4 *Example "Killer Phrases"*

also developed an evaluation instrument referred to as PIES (Preliminary Innovation Evaluation System) designed to help inventors evaluate the viability of their innovations.[7] Similar to NewProd™, PIES provides questions on the market, the competitive environment, and the product description. Although there is no one instrument that has proven reliable for all types of products, it is useful to examine different approaches to create a screening tool appropriate for your specific needs. These two approaches—NewProd™ and PIES—as well as others, strive to identify the key success factors that help identify potential winning concepts in the new product process.

Some example screening criteria for new products specify that they:

- provide unique benefits to customers
- have concrete advantages over the competition
- build on company strengths and competencies
- fit the strategic plan and direction for the company
- use existing channels and sales force (or provide an entrée to a new channel)
- can be produced in large volume (or require short runs)
- appeal to current loyal customers (or provide an entry to new customers)

---

7. An example of an early version of the innovation evaluation instrument can be found in the appendix of William Lesch and David Rupert, *New Product Screening: A Step-Wise Approach* (New York: The Haworth Press, 1994). Information on the assessment program offered by The Innovation Institute can be found at uiausa.com/UIAIAPi2.htm.

- provide a minimum ROI
- enable an acceptable payback period
- can be ordered and processed through existing IT capabilities

Once the most significant criteria are identified, you must decide whether they
will be used as concrete go/no go factors, or whether they will be used to comprise a tool for rating new product ideas. The grid in Figure 8.5 shows an example of a screening tool in which nine factors were determined to be important in
predicting new product success. The first criterion, fit in product mix, was given
a weight of 3. Since the first idea was given a rating of 1, the weighted rating for
the idea on this criterion was 3 (1×3). Similarly, the second idea was rated 3 for
a weighted score on this criterion of 9, and the third idea was rated 2 for a
weighted score of 6.

Concept Refinement and Specification of Requirements

The product manager is expected to provide the "voice of the customer" in the
new product development process. This means converting the raw data from customer needs into what the product is expected to do. Before writing these specifications, however, the product manager should take a step back to the new
product objectives to determine what corporate expectations the product or service is intended to meet. Will the new product, for example, provide inroads into
a desired market? What are your assumptions that support this statement? Are
there any constraints that may make it difficult for the new product to achieve
these objectives?

FIGURE 8.5 *Example Screening Checklist*

	WEIGHTED VALUE	IDEA 1		IDEA 2		IDEA 3	
Fit in product mix	**3**	1	3	3	9	2	6
Patentability							
Low risk of competition							
Existing channels							
Fit with strategy							
Payback of x years							
ROI of x%							
Tooling and machinery							
Core technologies							
	Total						

After the product scope is determined relative to the new product objectives, it's important to look at the total solution product (as described in Chapter 6) to ensure that requirements for all aspects of the solution are considered. For example, to simplify the installation of computer components by consumers, connecting cables are now color-coded. Although this had nothing to do with the functionality of the product, it required a change in requirements for the new product. Here are possible categories for which requirements might make sense for your product or service:

- product/service functionality
- manufacturing
- inventory
- shipping
- installation
- customer storage requirements
- interface with customer's products, services, systems, or capabilities
- safety
- physical design or appearance

As part of understanding the total solution, you must collect needs information from customers. Note that the needs are what the customer wants to get out of using the product (the benefits) rather than *how* the product is to be developed. Similar to the research during ideation, open-ended questions may be appropriate, but they are geared more to a defined concept. Rating scales and closed-ended questions may also be used.

The concept statement can come in many forms. Sometimes it is a verbal description of the product, explaining the differentiating characteristics. Other times, a picture or even rough prototype is more appropriate. If price is a significant factor in the customer's purchase decision, include it; otherwise, ignore it (in the concept statement). If price is an important criterion, the target price should be included in the customer research. Subtracting a desired margin from the price yields a target cost, a value that may have a direct impact on the product design, as shown in Figure 8.6.

Customers can be asked how unique they perceive the described concept compared with the competition, what they like and dislike about the product, what improvements they think are necessary, whether they would consider buying the product when available, and, if relevant, how much or how frequently they would buy. The questions on uniqueness and purchase intentions help refine the sales forecast (as mentioned earlier), whereas the questions on product attributes guide the development of product requirements. Ratings of specific attributes (again on a scale from very important to very unimportant) provide data necessary for moving closer to the ability to define the product characteristics more specifically.

The next step, therefore, is to convert this understanding of customer needs into verifiable product requirements. Similar to the need for SMART objectives (as described in Chapter 3), product managers should attempt to provide product requirements that are measurable and attainable. Knowing that customers want a product that is "user-friendly" or "portable" is insufficient. Rather than stating the need to be user-friendly, specify the maximum number of steps the customer will go through in using the product. Rather than specifying that the product be portable, specify the maximum weight, transport means, and/or other variables related to portability.[8]

Obviously, not all needs will have the same priorities. Some will be more important to customers than others, and some can be addressed by combining

---

8. See Ivy Hooks and Kristin Farry, *Customer-Centered Products* (New York: AMACOM, 2001) for a good discussion of developing solid requirements for new products. Chapter 10, in particular, highlights unverifiable words and possible substitutes.

FIGURE 8.6 *Using Target Price in Product Specifications*

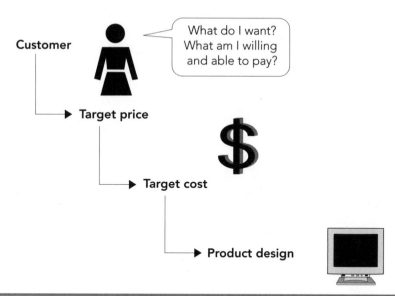

them into one requirements statement. Put the needs on sticky notes to group them into categories and eliminate redundancies. Then determine which needs are absolute and which would be "nice to have," based on what customers have told you. This will allow you to prioritize the needs without building in excess.

Determining attribute priorities and establishing target specifications are not yet the end of the process. The attributes must also be compared with the competition. If an attribute is highly important to the customers, product managers should strive to establish competitive superiority for that feature whenever possible. If an attribute has low importance, product managers should determine whether it can be eliminated to reduce costs, or if simply being as good as the competition is sufficient.

Although defining these high-level specifications may be appropriate for some products, others may depend on component and subcomponent requirements. Different members of the team might be responsible for different level product specifications (see Figure 8.7).

Product managers should ensure that the requirements from one level are linked to the other related levels. For example, a component or subcomponent of a new software product may be a module or capability of interfacing with competing products. Many companies already accomplish this task as a result of their quality control efforts, but it is not always automatic. When subcomponent

FIGURE 8.7 *Hierarchy of Product Requirements*

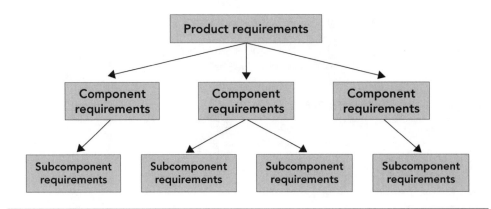

requirements, for example, don't link back to the high-level product requirements, it could mean that either a specific requirement is unnecessary, or it may mean that something was overlooked in the overall product specifications. In either case, the product manager should be aware of the discrepancy in case it affects the refined set of requirements.

This, then, leads to the final step—refinement. The product manager must consider the customer need priorities, the competitive performance benchmarks, and any linkages across different product development levels and then work with the team on the final set of product requirements that will be necessary for prototype development. Remember that the job of the product manager here is to supply sufficient detail about the benefits the product must provide without specifying the exact materials and design, which would be the job of the product designer.

In summary, the eight-step process of concept refinement and specification of requirements is as follows:

1. Revisit the new product objectives and assumptions as they relate to this concept.
2. List the "total solution" categories for which requirements should be made.
3. Determine customer needs and priorities.
4. Convert needs data into concrete target requirements.
5. Prioritize the needs for the "high-level" product requirements.
6. Compare with competitive benchmark specifications.
7. Establish hierarchy of requirements, with an understanding of linkages.
8. Refine the requirements.

Reflection Point

How effective am I in refining concepts and writing specifications?

- What new product objectives are related to this concept?
- How complete a solution do my new products provide to customers?

- How well do I link all levels of product requirements?
- Do my specifications bring in the voice of the customer?
- Do my specifications help with technical product design?

Prototype Testing

The purpose of prototype testing is to ensure that components and subsystems of the product work together as planned—commonly under real world conditions. Some tests may clarify customer product preferences (by providing something concrete for customers to react to), and others may define milestones by which management makes a decision to continue the project.[9] Although different terms might be applied in different companies, products to be tested might be referred to as experimental, alpha, beta, or preproduction prototypes. When both alpha and beta tests are used, an alpha test often refers to an internal, company-testing of the prototype. For example, a piece of financial software might be put to a test in the firm's accounting department, or a consumer product may be given to employees to use in their homes. A beta test refers to an external, customer-testing of the product. Some companies also use gamma tests, which refer to providing the product to key stakeholders (such as industry analysts and media representatives) who may be influential in providing a stamp of approval for the final launch.

There are very few proven guidelines for beta tests due to the variability in the usage of different products and services. Some beta tests are for a few days, others for months. Some may involve very few customers; others require thousands. Some products are given free to customers even after the test is complete, others require at least partial payment and/or return of the product at the conclusion of

---

9. See Chapter 10 of Karl Ulrich and Steven Eppinger, *Product Design and Development* (New York: McGraw-Hill, 1995) for a discussion of effective prototyping.

the test. Product managers must use common sense in deciding these factors. Issues that a product manager should consider in developing a beta test program include:

- What is the best demographic profile of beta product users? (This depends on your defined target market or markets.)
- How many beta test sites are necessary to provide acceptable information? (This depends on whether the prototype might be used differently or perform differently for different markets.)
- How long should the beta test be? (This depends on how long it would take for customers to thoroughly test it.)
- Who pays for the beta product, and how much should the payment be?
- Are there any risks to the beta user? If so, what can be done to minimize the risk?
- Will the beta user customers be significant sources of testimonials at the time of launch?
- How will confidentiality be handled?

Selection of the appropriate beta test site is important for assuring product quality and determining necessary modifications prior to launch. However, there are a few other factors implied by these questions. The right beta site can help with the launch by providing testimonials of value to the sales force and channel. Unfortunately, if the product does not function as promised, the relationship with the customer can be strained. If that happens, it has the potential to also strain the relationship between the product manager and the salesperson in whose territory this customer is located. That implies how critical it is for product managers to work carefully with the sales force to determine proper selection and care of the customer relationship.

KEY POINTS
- Clarify the new product objectives of your company.
- Maintain a continual stream of new product ideas.
- Use both reactive and proactive tools, and as many sources as possible, for new product ideas.
- Use and reconcile different approaches to forecasting.
- Develop a concrete business case for your new product.
- Avoid killer phrases.

Reflection Point

How effective am I in using prototype testing?

- What guidelines make sense for my product?
- How informed do I keep the salespeople whose customers are involved with the beta tests?

- Do I use the appropriate types of prototype testing?
- Do I obtain testimonials to help with the eventual launch of the product?

- Refine the criteria most appropriate for screening new product ideas in your firm.
- Obtain customer input on concepts and prototypes, as appropriate.
- If there is a hierarchy of product requirements, make certain all levels are consistent.
- Select beta test customers with care.

CONCEPT AND DEVELOPMENT CHECKLIST

NEW PRODUCT OBJECTIVES

Are your firm's new product objectives clear to you?	Yes	No
Have you related these objectives to your new product efforts?	Yes	No
Are you aware of the new product process used by your firm, including milestones, checkpoints, and sign-offs?	Yes	No

IDEA GENERATION

Do you have an ongoing pipeline of new product ideas at different stages of development?	Yes	No
Do your ideas ensure that corporate growth targets can be met?	Yes	No

CONCEPT AND DEVELOPMENT CHECKLIST, *continued*

Have you developed ideas for both new products and line extensions?	Yes	No
Do you use both internal and external sources of ideas?	Yes	No
Does your idea set represent a portfolio with varying degrees of risk?	Yes	No

FORECASTING AND CONCEPT TESTING

Are your forecasts built from several data points?	Yes	No
Do the forecasts take into account market friction?	Yes	No
Do your forecasts take into account cannibalization?	Yes	No
Does your forecast help you build a concrete business case?	Yes	No
Do you use appropriate criteria to screen out bad concepts while leaving in good concepts?	Yes	No
Do you continually refine your process of writing the business case?	Yes	No

CONCEPT REFINEMENT AND SPECIFICATION OF REQUIREMENTS

Have you explored the total solution from all angles prior to writing the product specifications?	Yes	No
Do you consider whether the final price will have a significant impact on potential product design features?	Yes	No
Do you write product requirements that are measurable and attainable?	Yes	No
Do your product requirements embody the voice of the customer?	Yes	No
If relevant, are all of the product requirement levels in sync?	Yes	No

CONCEPT AND DEVELOPMENT CHECKLIST, *continued*

PROTOTYPE TESTING

Have you identified the role of prototype testing in your process?   Yes   No

Have you considered all types of prototype testing to determine
what is most appropriate?   Yes   No

Have you fully defined the complete beta test program?   Yes   No

Have you involved any salespeople who have beta test sites in
their territories?   Yes   No

Have you gained commitment from the customers participating
in the beta test program to provide testimonials?   Yes   No

Launch Guidelines for New Products

"If you have tried to do something and failed, you are vastly better off than if you tried to do nothing and succeeded."

—Lloyd Jones, author

Product launch refers to the process of putting all the pieces together to get your product to market. This can include training the sales force and the channel, communicating to customers through advertising and public relations, and announcing the product internally. To be effective in the launch, a significant amount of preplanning must be done. Most of what is executed during the launch *should* be completed by pre-launch. In fact, if a product is launched to internal or external reps with a promise that various systems and marketing communications are *forthcoming* (rather than ready), that promise can have a damaging impact on the credibility of the launch. Therefore, this chapter drills into the many aspects of launch preparation as a predecessor to the actual launch activities, follows with implementing the launch, then briefly lists items that should be taken into consideration after the launch.

Launch Preparation: Start Early

New products and services are being delivered to the market at a staggering pace. And that sometimes causes products to be launched "before their time." Numerous decisions need to be made prior to the launch so that at the time of general availability (GA) the details have been completed. The basic pre-launch

PRE-LAUNCH PREPARATIONS

New product ground rules:	positioning and goals
Timing:	when to launch
Scope:	roll-out or full-scale
Ancillary issues:	packaging, warranty
Communications strategy:	course of action
Stakeholders:	who they are and what they need
Deadlines:	milestones, dates

considerations, as listed in the table above, are ground rules, timing, scope, ancillary issues, communications strategy, stakeholder involvement, and deadlines.

These seven issues should be evaluated carefully to increase the potential for success of a new product. They consume time and energy, especially since they require widespread buy-in. If launches are simply a marketing job, they won't work as well as when there is full commitment.

Clarify New Product Ground Rules

Most of the new product ground rules will have been established earlier in the new product development process, but it's useful to retrace them at the pre-launch phase to ensure that nothing has been overlooked. Strategy, target customers, positioning, and similar issues should be revisited to ensure clarity.

Understanding how the product fits in the overall corporate strategy is important for preparing the launch strategy. Some new products are designed to augment the corporate direction, whereas others are designed to change it. For example, new products may be targeted at customers in a different country or industry, requiring not just a new product but also changes in brand and communications strategies. Some products are stand-alone offerings, whereas others are relevant to customers only as part of a complete solution. If a product cannot stand alone, it may be wise to delay the launch until a complete solution is available for customers. Some products are substitutes to replace existing devices whereas others are complements or new and discrete offerings. When products are substitutes, the timing of launch can be critical to minimize overstock and out-of-stock situations.

Reflection Point

How does this new product "fit" in my firm's corporate, brand, and product strategies?

- What role does the product play in helping the company achieve its goals of growth and corporate identity?

- Should the product be branded separately, or should it be under the corporate "umbrella"?
- What are the product interdependencies? What strategies are necessary to improve the effectiveness of the overall product line?

Determine where this product fits in the overall "road map" for the product family. Is it part of an existing or new platform? Can past successes be leveraged? Is there a need to de-emphasize certain aspects of functionality? If you are dealing with a technology or medical product, how well does it fit with industry standards? Is compatibility with existing equipment or software a concern for customers? If there were beta tests, did they provide any data that could be useful here?

Finally, take a look at the resources for the launch. Check whether the budget and capacity will allow the product to achieve its goals, or whether revisions are going to be necessary.

Defining the target customers should include, but go beyond, a description of SIC (Standard Industrial Classification) codes or demographic profiles of buyers. Start with a listing of job titles, responsibilities, and company types and sizes for B2B products (or demographics such as age, sex, income, education, and marital status for consumer products). Then carry this analysis to a higher level. Ask yourself if you have identified all of the buying points including influencers, users, and decision makers. The value proposition for a CEO will likely be different from the value proposition for an engineer or a department head. Then determine whether you truly understand the various types of value for your new product. Who are the primary and secondary markets for sales and advertising messages? How will the messages differ? Determine whether the primary prospects are new or existing customers, as well as the resulting impact that will have on launch. Salespeople can benefit from a psychographic description of target customers, including applications, benefits, competitive products, and risk-taking profile. Visualize the customer as a person or an account rather than simply as a

Reflection Point

What is the profile of the "best" customer for this product?

- What problem(s) is the product designed to solve?

- What is the value proposition for this customer, as well as for other buying points?

"market." What is the job description for your prospect? If the best prospect profile matches the beta test customer, use that as a beginning point for your description.

Included in the new product ground rules are the positioning and financial goals established earlier in the process. *Positioning* refers to defining where the product fits within the market and against competitors. What advantage does this product have over both the competition and over internal products it has been designed to replace? Is the advantage due to product features or to the image and support of the company? Does superiority exist? Is it clear to the customers? Which customers benefit most? The greater the advantage (perceived and real) is over the competition, the greater the chances of new product success. Even though advantage is partly subjective and partly objective, it should be articulated. The positioning statement for the product should clarify who the competition is, how this new product is better, and what substantiation exists to prove the superiority.

Sometimes the research that was conducted on the market is several years old by the time the product is ready to launch. The product manager has to determine whether the information is still valid or whether new research needs to be obtained. Have customer needs changed? Has the set of competitive offerings changed? Is the price point still valid?

Clarify the Timing

The question of when to launch a new product can vary in importance depending on the industry. The timing of the new product launch relative to the competition, relative to your own product line, and relative to other factors is influenced by many issues and should be explored.

Reflection Point

What is the competitive positioning of this product?

- Is there verifiable superiority?

- Has the positioning been updated as necessary throughout the process?

If given a choice, most companies prefer to bring out a new product in advance of the competition. However, there are advantages and disadvantages to launching before, after, or at the same time as the competition. Launching a product before the competition is desirable when it allows you to build barriers through continual improvement and establish a premier position. On the other hand, in many instances the "fast follower" gains the advantage by learning from the innovator's mistakes and capitalizing on them. And finally, in situations where a new-to-the-world product is being introduced, it may be beneficial for the competitors to launch at the same time to share the costs of "educating" the market. Since it is difficult, at best, to precisely time your launch relative to the competition, this aspect of timing is quite broad but nevertheless worth conceptualizing as part of the overall launch strategy.

Decisions regarding timing should consider what impact the new product may have on the rest of the product line. As mentioned earlier, launching a product before components essential to its usability are available is premature timing. Similarly, launching substitute products must be appropriately timed. If there is substantial pipeline inventory in the channel, you may desire to postpone the launch until some of the old product has been sold. On the other hand, if a delayed launch risks a vacuum period when there is no inventory of either the old or the new product, it can create a period of potential advantage for the competition. In that case, plan a period of overlap, using pricing and/or channel strategy to differentiate the substitutes and minimize cannibalization.

You may also want to look at the launch of other new products in your own company. How much time should be between launches? Companies with a reputation of being innovative may want to maintain a constant stream of new products, and too much of a delay could be perceived negatively. On the other hand, if your launch occurs too close to another product's launch, there may be a reduction on the effectiveness of one or both launches.

Reflection Point

What is the best timing for the launch of this product?

- Are there any forthcoming competitive launches to consider?
- What impact will this new product have on my existing products? Will that affect the timing of the launch?
- What impact do seasonality, customer purchase cycles, or trade shows have on the timing of the launch?

Timing of the launch may also be influenced by several practical factors such as seasonality, customer purchase cycles, and the importance of new product trade shows. If a product is not ready to hit these particular time-sensitive events, a decision will need to be made whether to delay the launch until the next relevant event, or to launch it independent of the timing issues.

Clarify the Scope

In a perfect world, new products are launched to the entire target market at once. However, there are several situations where a rollout may be preferred to a full-scale launch. First, your firm may not have the capacity to meet the potential demand of the entire market; therefore, prioritizing market entry may be required. Second, cash flow may be a concern; a rollout strategy would provide earlier cash flow to fund penetration into other markets. Finally, a rollout strategy can reduce risk and allow you to learn throughout the commercialization process. The downside, however, is that a rollout strategy could put you at the mercy of a competitor who is initiating a full-scale launch of a competing product.

To plan your rollout strategy you should consider how to best prioritize the markets. Do you want to start with the most attractive markets in terms of size and dollar potential? Or might it be desirable to enter markets where competition is weak, providing an ability to gain experience, exposure, and market position? The segmentation can be done geographically, or by industry or application. For example, an international rollout process could start with the United States, then move to select countries in Europe and Asia, before entering industrializing nations. A domestic rollout might start in major metropolitan areas or in specific regions of high customer concentration. Similarly, a company may prioritize industries or applications. For example, a nutritional food product may start with hospitals and healthcare institutions before rolling out into commercial and retail applications.

Channel influence may also affect your rollout strategy. There may be key distributors or retailers who can provide both the cash flow and serve as catalysts for subsequent sales. Which channels and channel members are most critical to your new product's success, and what are your plans to motivate them? Ask yourself how prospects would likely want to buy this product. What role might the Internet play? Are existing reps and distributors appropriate to reach the right customers for this product? Are the selected channels appropriate for the price point position of the product? Are they capable of providing adequate support?

To prioritize the rollout sequence, it may be useful to rank the potential markets (industries, regions, etc.) according to significant criteria as indicated in the following evaluation table.

Evaluation of Potential Rollout Markets

	MARKET A	MARKET B	MARKET C	MARKET D	MARKET E
Sales potential					
Local reputation					
Pipeline inventory					
Competition					
Overall rank					

Clarify the Ancillary Issues

New product success can be influenced by the total package of the product—packaging, warranty, and supporting services. These cannot be afterthoughts, but should rather be planned up front during the development and pre-launch. Packaging can serve several purposes: protecting the product; enhancing the positioning; and facilitating storage, use, convenience, or recycling. Packaging can conceivably be part of the total solution desired by customers. Under what conditions might your customers store this product? Is water resistance, stackable strength, or dimensional compactness important to them? Do customers

Reflection Point

Should I initiate a full-scale launch or a rollout?

- Can a rollout approach improve my cash flow or establish a halo effect from positive sales to lead distributors or customers?

- What should be the entry sequence for the rollout and why?
- What changes should I consider in channel design and selection?

want individually packaged products, or do they prefer to buy in bulk? Is your customer base interested in "green" packaging to protect the environment? Product documentation can be an important ancillary item for technical or complex products. The documentation may contain product specifications, user (or owner) manuals, configuration guides, and related support materials. Is this documentation available? Is it free of internal jargon and unnecessary complexity for easy use by the intended audience?

A superior warranty program can sometimes provide a competitive advantage (or overcome a perceived disadvantage), but only if it is well planned and well executed. A number of questions should be addressed when designing the warranty. How long should the warranty period be and why? Who is eligible to receive the warranty? What will trigger the warranty? What will be provided (replacement, repair, cash) when a warranty claim is submitted? What are the components of competitive warranties?

Supporting services may also influence the acceptance of and satisfaction with new products. Is third-party installation important to your target market, or will a technical hotline and website suffice? Is training in place (or completed) for these service providers? What other types of advice might be important to your target customers? Is customization necessary, desired by the market, and/or offered by the competition? Are processes already in place to provide the supporting services?

All of these ancillary materials should be launched with the product. Announcing the availability of the product externally (including to the sales force) without having the complete system or total product available can sometimes harm the company more than if the product were not launched at all.

Reflection Point

What ancillary products or services are necessary for this product to be successful?

- How might I use packaging to increase competitive advantage?

- How might I use warranty to increase competitive advantage?
- What additional services would strengthen the new product potential?

Clarify the Communications Strategy

The message and media strategy for a new product launch will follow many of the general issues for marketing communications (as will be discussed in Chapter 11), but some of the issues most critical to a new product launch strategy will be mentioned here. When possible, public relations and publicity should be the first step in the new product communications strategy and should *precede* the launch date. The more differentiated and unique the product, the more valuable is the public relations effort. *Public relations* refers to the activities and events a company stages to attain media visibility. These can include, but are not limited to, open houses, tours, speeches, and sponsorships. The information presented in the media about these events, as well as the publishing of articles and press releases, is *publicity*.

Public relations and publicity should be the first communications tools used for products that offer unique benefits to customers. (In other words, these tools will generally be most effective for products that are more than minimally different line extensions or cost reduction efforts.) For example, when Lipitor (a cholesterol-lowering drug developed by Warner Lambert) was in the final stages of testing by the FDA, it teamed with the American Heart Association in a national cholesterol education program. Through this public relations effort, the company positioned itself as being concerned about high cholesterol, thereby providing a solid position for the emergence of Lipitor.

There are other components a product manager can incorporate into a new product public relations campaign.

1. Develop press kits to be used at trade shows and other events. At minimum, these kits should contain beta test results (if available); white papers

detailing the importance of the new product; corporate history, positioning, and background information; and copies of press releases.

2. Draft articles for select publications explaining how their readers will benefit from this new product. For publishers to be interested in these types of articles, the product must be truly novel, and the article must provide information value to the reader beyond a sales pitch.

3. Again, if the product is truly innovative, it may be possible to provide a demonstration as part of an educational session at a trade show.

4. Issue press releases to appropriate media.

After public relations opportunities are exhausted, it's time to begin advertising in earnest. Although the public relations activities often precede the launch date, most of the advertising and other promotional activities coincide with launch. To be sure that happens, the planning must be completed prior to launch.

In general, the advertising or marketing communications for a new product launch will contain objectives, a message strategy, and a media strategy. The objectives state what you want the advertising to do for your new product. Are you trying to create awareness? If so, state the objective quantitatively as in: "within three months of launch 40 percent of the target market will be aware of the availability of Product X" or "within ten months 30 percent of the market will be aware that the new product will extend the life of their equipment." If the goal of the campaign is to stimulate trial, state an objective such as: "to attain trial by 25 percent of the target market."

To define your target market, go back to your "best prospect" profile; then determine the most critical benefit to emphasize. This will be the focus for your message strategy. Lead the communications with *this* benefit for *this* particular market. Be sure to address the following in the communication. What will your product (service) do for the prospect? How will it do that? Why is it better than the competition? What proof do you have to make your claims credible? What can the prospects do if they are not satisfied with the purchase? Note that the first question identifies the benefit, the second question provides the features that supply the benefit, and the third question demonstrates the advantages.

This technique contains the same components as the typical FAB (Features, Advantages, Benefits) approach to sales training, but reorganizes them (into BFA) so that benefits are the most important and first thing presented to the prospect. The product manager is responsible for translating the positioning strategy mentioned earlier into a communications message for the customers, and for keeping the message relevant and current. Be sure to capture testimonials from any beta sites that may be useful in the launch. Then the product manager determines the best media strategy to convey the message: through trade shows, through the sales force and/or channels, through print media, through direct mail, through electronic transmission, or through other means. Targeted advertising in trade journals to coincide with the launch of the product at a trade show can be effective. Try to get your message in front of prospects multiple times through creative use of potential media.

Direct salespeople will need various types of communications materials including internal (confidential) company information, sales tools they can use on calls, and marketing collateral they can give to customers. The internal documentation contains the product's sales objectives and positioning, along with competitive comparisons and very likely proprietary data. (This information may be placed on the corporate intranet as well as be distributed in print format.) The sales tools should be focused on helping the salespeople complete the sales call; therefore, the emphasis should be on *how to sell*. The collateral pieces should be written from the customer's perspective, following the BFA approach mentioned earlier. (If the target is a distributor, the material should focus on how the distributor will benefit from the product. If the target is an end user, the material should focus on end user benefits.) Even when the customer is an end user, different types of benefits may be relevant depending on the individual's level. Top managers, for example, are interested in how the new product will impact their bottom lines, whereas technical people may be more interested in datasheets. Too often, product managers provide only product features and benefits (relevant to technical people) and don't provide supporting material for salespeople to use for higher-level managers.

Communications materials for indirect sales channels will have some differences. The company information will be focused more on the partnership or relationship between the manufacturer and the distributor and will not contain the confidential information. For high-margin products, videos and electronic self-testing modules may be beneficial—but only if the channel perceives a true value in the time commitment. The sales tools will likely be shorter, with less detail. The collateral pieces should focus on end user benefits. The percentage of the budget devoted to communications material for direct versus indirect channels will depend on the channel prioritization that is part of the launch strategy.

Clarify the Stakeholder Issues

Although most stakeholders have been involved throughout the development process, here is another opportunity to be sure no one was overlooked prior to the launch. Generally, R&D, manufacturing, and marketing have been intimately

Reflection Point

How effectively have I integrated marketing communications for the launch?

- How can I increase public relations and publicity?
- Do the marketing communications make the product's advantages visible?

- Where can I be most effective and efficient in getting my message to the right prospects?
- What changes can I make in support materials to make them more useful for the sales force? For indirect channels?

involved in the development process and are cognizant of the targeted launch date. However, there may be others less "in tune" with the dates. Customer service should have the targeted date for release of the new product, along with scripts of answers to questions they may receive. The information technology (IT) group should be in the loop to ensure that accounting and ordering systems are in place, or will be at the time of launch. (It is very frustrating for a customer to become excited about a new product and then be unable to purchase it due to process inefficiencies from the manufacturer.) If the advertising department or agency has not been involved throughout the process (which they should have been), they must quickly be brought up to speed at this point. Any industry analysts or opinion leaders who have not yet been exposed to the new product should be notified. Key distributors that are going to be priorities in a rollout strategy must be aware of the launch date. (If new contracts or contract changes are necessary for the new product launch, these should also be available for the distributors at this point.) Technical support should be trained and ready for the product launch.

Clarify the Launch Deadlines and Milestones

There may be a number of events and activities that will happen between now and launch—some may already be part of the project plan while others may still need to be added. In either case, establishing a milestone activities chart can be a useful trigger or reminder of what still needs to be done.

The *milestone activities chart* lists the desired dates of completion for significant activities such as purchasing equipment for the launch, finalizing package

Reflection Point

What have I done to ensure that all relevant stakeholders have been considered prior to the launch?

- Is training important for any of these stakeholders?

Reflection Point

What processes and procedures can I institute to help me avoid overlooking deadlines and milestones?

- Have I consolidated all relevant dates from other activities into a milestone activities chart?

design, obtaining legal clearance, subcontracting specialized labor, and preparing the owner's manual. Each of these may require several steps and may vary in importance depending on the project. Their potential impact on product success must be considered when assessing priority. For example, electronic or high-tech consumer products require clarity in technical documentation to be successful and therefore require high priority. The format of the milestone activities chart can vary from a simple list of activities and dates to more formal project schedule and control techniques like Gantt and PERT charts. Many of the project management principles applied to the product development process can be adapted to the launch process as well.

PRE-LAUNCH CHECKLIST

NEW PRODUCT STRATEGY

Is the product consistent with the corporate identity?	Yes	No
Does the product help attain corporate goals?	Yes	No

PRE-LAUNCH CHECKLIST, *continued*

Has the product been fit into a product road map?	Yes	No
Have you developed an ideal customer profile?	Yes	No
Is there a clear and verifiable superiority in the competitive positioning?	Yes	No
Do current customer and competitor data still validate the original product goals?	Yes	No

TIMING
Is the target launch date the best possible timing?	Yes	No

SCOPE
Has a careful rollout strategy been developed?	Yes	No
Are the reasons for the rollout strategy valid?	Yes	No

ANCILLARY ISSUES
Is product documentation complete and available?	Yes	No
If appropriate, is the warranty program finalized?	Yes	No
Are all supporting services ready and available?	Yes	No

COMMUNICATIONS STRATEGY
Have you exhausted all possible publicity outlets?	Yes	No
Are your marketing communications directed at the best prospect profile?	Yes	No
Are communication materials for the direct and indirect sales forces designed to help sell?	Yes	No
Are these materials ready?	Yes	No
Have you obtained testimonials, case analyses, or other customer statements regarding the use/benefits of the product?	Yes	No

PRE-LAUNCH CHECKLIST, *continued*

STAKEHOLDERS
Have you identified and notified all stakeholders?   Yes   No

DEADLINES AND MILESTONES
Have you consolidated the dates of important deadlines and
activities into a milestone activities chart?   Yes   No

Implement the Launch: Establish Buy-In and Support

Sometimes the product announcement is considered the culmination of the launch, but it's really just the beginning. Implementing the launch requires putting the pre-launch plans into action, including gaining awareness of, stocking, and trial purchase of the product. This requires training and motivating the people responsible for executing the launch plan.

One of the most critical pre-launch actions to take is to ensure product readiness. Be sure that all of the ancillary and communications issues—both internal and external—have been addressed. Also, verify that systems are in place for ordering and supporting the product once it is released. Then, if you haven't already done so, work with sales administration, human resources, or any other departments in charge of training to prepare the educational processes related to launch.

Internal Training

Companies have realized that new product training should encompass customer service, technical support, and other customer-contact positions (in addition to sales). People in these positions can have a pronounced impact on new product success (or failure). Although they may not need the depth of "how-to-sell" information that is provided to the sales force, they should know what the importance of the product is to the company, who will provide what types of support to the customer, and how to answer expected questions.

FIGURE 9.1 *Avoid the Product Presentation Training*

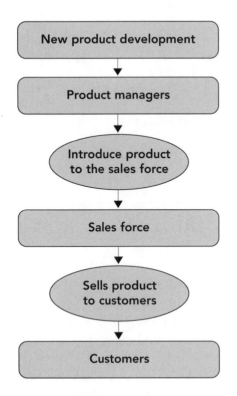

1 New product sales kit is prepared based on product capabilities and superiorities.

2 Product managers provide training on product's "bells and whistles."

3 Sales force learns product-centered information about capabilities, competitive superiorities, etc.

4 Sales force sells product to customers as it was communicated to them—in terms of product capabilities.

That being said, effectively motivating the sales force to sell a new product can spell the difference between success and failure. But one of the problems with much of the sales training conducted for new products is that the focus is more on what the product *does* than how it benefits the customer.

The purpose of training is to prepare the field sales force to sell the product, as well as know the product. The bulk of information presented should focus the salespeople on their customers rather than internally. Why doesn't this happen? Product managers have lived in a development mindset for so long, building in features to differentiate the product from the competition, that they can't wait to dazzle the sales force with the brilliance of its superior capabilities. Simply providing benefits doesn't solve this problem since the true focus is still on features. Product training and sales skill training need to merge with regard to new products. The product-centered training looks something like the flowchart in Figure 9.1.

Salespeople need the profile of the ideal customer, as discussed earlier. What is the current situation for the customer that this product is designed to improve

FIGURE 9.2 *Replace Product Presentation Training with Need-Centered Training*

1 Prepare customer-centered training process.

Prepare ideal customer profile with description of current situation.

2 List actual or potential customers along with success stories from beta sites and preliminary sales.

Identify target customers.

3 Change from FAB to BFA presentation.

Introduce product to salespeople in terms of its problem-solving capabilities.

4 Plan a call in terms of questions to uncover customer problems and needs.

Plan role-playing that initially never mentions the product.

5 Conduct a dry run using role-playing and discussions.

Role-play and test the call plan.

6 Plan a call for each strategically important customer type.

Plan calls to other key customer segments and types.

or change? What improvements or changes are desired? Why (and how badly) do customers want these changes? How will they objectively judge whether your product can indeed provide the desired results?

Unfortunately, too many product managers list all markets that might or could buy the new product in an attempt to build enthusiasm for its many applications. This shotgun approach dilutes the sales efforts rather than points to opportunities with the highest probability of payback. When salespeople start with the best prospects and generate some hits, sales revenue will flow faster and reps will be more committed to the product.

Changing the training to focus on the customer, the customer's business, and the customer needs will increase the effectiveness of the sales force. As part of the training, the sales force should receive a new product kit comprised of the internal information, sales tools, and marketing collateral described earlier in this chapter. The new training should look something like the flowchart in Figure 9.2.

A need-centered training approach as conveyed in Figure 9.2 is the first step in motivating the sales force. However, the sales force will also want to know the

Reflection Point

What improvements can I make in internal training for the launch?

- Have all people requiring training been identified and trained?

- Does the launch address both the educational "how-to-sell" needs of the sales force as well as the sales administration needs related to motivation?
- Can the salespeople make the product's advantages visible to customers?

"sales administration" details of the launch. Will they receive additional compensation (bonuses or higher commission) for selling the new product? How long will the higher compensation be in effect? What impact will this have on their quota? How will sales efforts be tracked?

Channel Motivation

Distributors, dealers, and other resellers don't have the same vested interest in the new product that internal stakeholders might. Yet they all play a crucial role in getting the product to target customers. Not only do these resellers need to believe it is a good business decision to make an investment in your new product, they must also be motivated to create the best environment to make the product a success. What training will their salespeople need? Will they need to provide technical training to their support personnel? How much inventory is necessary? Does the new product require minimum shelf space or specific shelf facings to be successful? Will the reseller need help promoting the product?

Distributors will be motivated to promote the new product if they believe it will increase their revenue or margin, or if they believe you will help them improve the efficiency of their business. They must trust that you have an outstanding product and that you will stand behind it. Some of the tools you can use to help motivate channel members are listed here.

TOOLS FOR MOTIVATING DISTRIBUTORS
1. Increase the distributor's revenue.
   - Advertise to the end customer to increase brand "pull."

   • Offer temporary product exclusivity or selectivity.
   • Provide merchandising assistance to increase sales.
2. Increase the distributor's margin.
   • Temporarily raise the basic percentage margin.
   • Provide new product allowances for promoting the product.
   • Offer to prepay the allowances.
3. Improve the efficiency of the distributor's business.
   • Provide business training (management, inventory, finance, marketing skills, etc.) to improve the distributor's operation.
   • Provide dollars to use for other sales skill training.
   • Drop-ship the new product to the distributor's customer.
   • Send prequalified leads to the distributor.
   • Assist in repackaging the product to fit space limitations.
4. Reduce the risk to the distributor of carrying the product.
   • Provide initial product training at no or reduced cost.
   • Demonstrate proof of customer acceptance of the product.
   • Offer a temporary returned goods policy that exceeds the norm.
   • Accomplish corporate preselling of the product (e.g., through advertising, trade shows, and other communications).

Customer Acceptance

Gaining customer acceptance (primarily in the form of trial) is the immediate goal of early launch. Awareness is the first step in the process toward acceptance and is the result of your earlier efforts in marketing communications, sales training, and channel motivation. The next step is customer trial.

There are different ways a customer might try your product. For small, low unit-margin items such as consumer-packaged goods, samples can be used to

---

Reflection Point

How can I increase the probability of getting customers to try the new product?	• Can I enable customers to sample the product without immediately committing to purchase? • What training activities might increase customer acceptance?

---

encourage trial. For larger items, other forms of trial may be more appropriate. Products are frequently put "on test" at a subsegment of a customer's business—such as one facility or location, a limited production run, or limited-time utilization. This reduces the risk to customers by allowing them to sample the product without making a total commitment to replacing all existing products with the new product. Some products, such as capital equipment, cannot be tried on a sample basis such as this. In those cases, companies develop "virtual" trials such as test-drives or intra-factory tests. For example, prospects might test-drive a new fire engine or bulldozer. Or a printing equipment manufacturer might take on customer print jobs to demonstrate the capabilities of new printing equipment. In other cases, video demonstrations or tours of beta sites might be necessary.

Customers may also need to be trained on the product, especially when they handle their own installation or repair. Training should focus on how to best integrate the product into their existing operations; how to deal with process differences; and how to reduce the time, cost, and energy of switching to the new product. Customer training can come in many forms: hands-on training provided as part of a product purchase (either free or for a fee), educational seminars (the white papers of education), and executive seminars by invitation only.

Early Performance Tracking

Although an ultimate metric of new product success will be sales, the sooner you can identify potential problems, the better it will be to take corrective action. That means you will want to track indicators that precede sales. For example, if it takes four sales calls on average to get a sale, monitor how many sales are being made on the new product. To encourage salespeople to make calls on the new product it may be necessary to initially (temporarily) provide incentives for a behavior (making appropriate sales calls) rather than for results (sales).

Reflection Point

What metrics, if tracked, could help me identify the trend toward success of the new product without waiting for sales results?

- Can the appropriate sales calls help predict future success?
- Is product placement in the channel related to sales?
- What role does awareness play?

Product placement on retail or distributor shelves may be another metric to track. What percent of distributors (or retailers) are stocking the product? What percent of those are giving it appropriate shelf space? Is demonstration or showroom visibility important? How effective are channel members in these areas?

Awareness of the new product among customers is another factor that has to precede sales. Measuring the awareness will require some sort of customer survey, but it may provide some critical insights into the future success of the new product. Sometimes tracking the communications plan against actual results can indicate potential corrective action. How many press releases were actually published? What was the result of product demonstrations at trade shows? Were ads placed as planned, and what readership results are available from the media reps?

LAUNCH IMPLEMENTATION CHECKLIST

INTERNAL TRAINING

Have all relevant employees been trained on the new product?	Yes	No
Does the sales training teach salespeople how to *sell* the product, as well as *know* the product?	Yes	No
Does the sales training focus more on the customers than on the product?	Yes	No
Have incentive programs been developed for, and communicated to, salespeople?	Yes	No

LAUNCH IMPLEMENTATION CHECKLIST, *continued*

Are new product sales kits ready and available for the sales force?	Yes	No
Are demos available and ready for the sales force?	Yes	No

CHANNEL MOTIVATION

Have technical training and sales training on the new product been offered to distributors/resellers?	Yes	No
Are incentive programs ready?	Yes	No
Is merchandising assistance and promotional support available?	Yes	No
Have resellers been provided with proof of the product's potential?	Yes	No

CUSTOMER ACCEPTANCE

Have marketing communications been used to presell the new product and gain initial awareness?	Yes	No
Have you provided opportunities for trial?	Yes	No
Is training available, as needed, for customers?	Yes	No

EARLY PERFORMANCE TRACKING

Have you identified metrics that can be used to help predict future sales?	Yes	No
Do you have a system for tracking these metrics?	Yes	No
Are you tracking actual communications activities against plan?	Yes	No

Post-Launch Tracking: Early Course Correction

After the product is launched, the process is not yet complete. It is important both to continue to track the success of the new product and to be prepared with contingency plans if necessary. This is referred to as a launch control system.

Finally, it is important to conduct an audit of the overall process to make improvements for the next major new product development effort.

With regard to initiating the launch control system, you can track several possible measures to determine the success of the product:

- unit sales
- returns
- discounts
- customer acceptance
- competitive response
- service calls
- shareholder value

The product manager must (1) determine which measures will best help spot potential problems, (2) design a tracking system, and (3) determine the frequency of tracking. This information is used to develop a control plan as shown here:

Sample Control Plan

POTENTIAL PROBLEM	TRACKING	CONTINGENCY PLAN
Salespeople fail to contact general-purpose market at a prescribed rate.	Track weekly call reports. The plan calls for at least 10 general-purpose calls per week per rep.	If activity falls below this level for three weeks running, a remedial program of one-day district sales meetings will be held.
Salespeople may fail to understand how the new feature of the product relates to product usage in the general-purpose market.	Tracking will be done by having sales manager call one rep each day. Entire sales force will be covered in two months.	Clarification will be given to individual reps on the spot, but if first 10 calls suggest a widespread problem, special teleconference calls will be arranged to repeat the story to the whole sales force.

Sample Control Plan, continued

POTENTIAL PROBLEM	TRACKING	CONTINGENCY PLAN
Potential customers are not making trial purchases of the product.	Track by instituting a series of 10 follow-up telephone calls a week to prospects who have received sales presentations. There must be 25 percent agreement on a product's main feature and trial orders from 30 percent of those prospects who agree on the feature.	Remedial plan provides for follow-up telephone sales calls to all prospects by reps, offering a 50 percent discount on all first-time purchases.
Buyers make trial purchase but do not place quantity reorders.	Track another series of telephone survey calls, this time to those who placed an initial order. Sales forecast based on 50 percent of trial buyers reordering at least 10 more units within six months.	No remedial plan for now. If customer does not rebuy, there is some problem in product use. Since product is clearly better, we must know the nature of the misuse. Field calls on key accounts will be used to determine that problem, and appropriate action will follow.
Chief competitor may have the same new feature (for which we have no patent) ready to go and markets it.	This situation is essentially untrackable. Inquiry among our suppliers and media will help us learn more quickly.	Remedial plan is to pull out all stops on promotion for 60 days. A make-or-break program. Full field selling on new item only, plus a 50 percent first-order discount and two special mailings. The other trackings listed above will be monitored even more closely.

Source: C. Merle Crawford, *New Products Management*, 4e (Burr Ridge, Ill.: Irwin, 1994) p. 317.

Reflection Point

What have I done to be able to expedite corrective action, if necessary, after the product launch?

- Have I established a launch control system?

- Do I evaluate the new product *process* as well as the new product itself?

Sometimes a revision of the marketing strategy can set the new product back on track. This could include repositioning, repackaging, bundling or unbundling, changing price, identifying new markets or customers, changing channels, or partnering with another company.

In other cases the product strategy itself must be modified. This could include revising the product, temporarily pulling the product out of the market, abandoning the product permanently, or selling the rights to the product.

The last part of the post-launch activities will be to evaluate the overall product development process. What worked especially well? What problems did the project team(s) face and why? What did we learn that we could apply to improve the product development process in the future?

KEY POINTS
- Start preparing for the launch early in the product development process.
- Complete the pre-launch checklist to ensure that you haven't overlooked items of importance.
- Prepare to establish buy-in and support from others in your organization.
- Complete the launch implementation checklist to determine whether there are launch components you still need to address.
- Establish a control plan to help you track the process of the launch.
- Complete the post-launch checklist.

POST-LAUNCH CHECKLIST

PRODUCT DEVELOPMENT PROCESS ISSUES

Was the new product delivered on time?	Yes	No
Was the project on budget?	Yes	No
Were all significant deadlines met?	Yes	No
Has a tracking system been developed to monitor product progress?	Yes	No
Has a control system been developed?	Yes	No
Should the existing process be used as is for future products?	Yes	No

MARKETING ISSUES

Are customers using the product as originally intended?	Yes	No
Have sales invoices been reviewed during the initial launch phase?	Yes	No
Have the price, discounts, and/or trade allowances been consistent and acceptable?	Yes	No
Was the product successfully positioned?	Yes	No
Was the product message clear in the mind of the customer?	Yes	No
Were support tools effective?	Yes	No
Has the competitive response been monitored and responded to?	Yes	No

POST-LAUNCH CHECKLIST, *continued*

INTERNAL ISSUES

Was the funding sufficient for the size of the project?	Yes	No
Did the project meet payback/return objectives?	Yes	No
Has the product met anticipated sales objectives?	Yes	No
Will the product meet the first quarter/year/long-term objectives?	Yes	No
Was the product sufficiently planned for, stocked, inventoried, and shipped?	Yes	No
Were there sufficient resources to place orders, manage customer orders, and effectively invoice customers?	Yes	No
Was production able to meet demand?	Yes	No

10

Pricing Frameworks and Tactics

"Price is the weapon of choice for many companies in the competition for sales and market share. However, the advantage is often short-lived and managers rarely balance the long-term consequences of deploying the price weapon against the likely short-term gains. . . ."

—Reed Holden and Thomas Nagle, coauthors, *The Strategy and Tactics of Pricing*[1]

Pricing is a "moment of truth" whereby product managers find out whether they are able to capture the value they have created in their products, services, and marketing programs. Since pricing strategy is the interface between finance and marketing, it requires a balance between cost management and market value, and it is driven by a corporate pricing posture. Some firms, such as Wal-Mart, strive for everyday low pricing (EDLP), and individual product prices reflect that. Others may want to maintain a premium position as a price leader and generally use higher prices to reflect that position. Still others prefer to be positioned slightly above or below the competition.

Pricing Goals and Objectives

In general, product managers should price their products to be consistent with the corporate price position or strategy, which may be a stated goal of their pricing. However, there could be many other goals, as listed here.

---

1. From the website of the Strategic Pricing Group, spgboston.com.

EXAMPLE PRICING GOALS OR OBJECTIVES

- maintain a price leadership position
- maintain an EDLP position
- discourage competition
- maximize short-term profits
- maximize long-term profits
- increase market share
- stabilize the market
- move weak items
- maintain channel loyalty
- avoid government intervention
- build traffic
- enhance company or product image

From a conceptual framework, pricing strategy results from an understanding of costs, customers, and competition (generally known as the three Cs of pricing). The cost of a product or service sets the floor for pricing decisions. But what is the true cost of a product? As discussed in Chapter 5, the way a firm accounts for its variable, direct, and allocated fixed costs can have a significant impact on the stated cost. In the long run all costs must be covered for a firm to stay in business. Consequently, the average price has to exceed the average total cost (i.e., full unit cost) of a product to be profitable. This full unit cost becomes the floor for long-term pricing decisions.

However, many pricing decisions are made in the short run. Should you change price in response to a competitive move? What price should be bid for a particular job? In these cases the variable costs of the product and incremental costs of the job set the floor for the pricing decision. Note that the cost floor does not dictate or suggest an optimal price, but rather identifies the point below which the price should not go. (There are obviously exceptions: when a product is perishable or obsolete, there may be a need to sell it below cost simply to get it out of inventory and avoid future expenses.) Numerous variables beyond cost would be examined to set the actual price.

The value that various customers place on your offering is another consideration in pricing. What is that value? Is it the same for all customers? Does it vary across time? What features or aspects of your products and services command the most value? What can you do to capture (through price) the varied components of value? This concept of value is the ceiling for the price you can charge.

Reflection Point

What is the pricing "posture" of my company?

- How does the umbrella pricing strategy of the company relate to my products?

- What goals or objectives are relevant for my products?
- How can I improve the cost management of my product area?
- Where can I get more detail on customers and competitors as it relates to pricing decisions?

The level of competitive prices, as well as the reactions of competitors to your pricing strategy, should also be studied. The competitive prices provide a benchmark against which customers compare your price. It's important, therefore, to know which competitors you are compared with and what your positioning is against them.

Beyond this conceptual discussion of the three Cs of pricing, product managers are concerned with making specific product pricing decisions such as how to price new products and line extensions and what factors to consider in making these decisions. They are also interested in dealing with issues such as how to:

- capture the value of supplementary services and options
- cope with price erosion in the industry
- change prices
- manage sales force discounting
- develop standard discount schedules
- respond to global pricing issues

The remainder of the chapter deals with these product pricing issues as well as policy, tactic, and decision issues.

New Product Pricing

Price estimation projects for new products may take several months. High sales potential products—especially those with high risk—will require a multidisciplinary project as discussed in Chapter 2, following a formal marketing research methodology as discussed in Chapter 4. The project will include researching competitors (to estimate their costs and assess pricing policies or strategies) and target customers (to determine their reaction to the proposed product and their willingness to buy at various price points).

The difficulty of researching new product prices increases with the degree of "newness." Products that are simple line extensions benefit from a pricing history of other products in the line. These "me-too" products can start the pricing evaluation from that of the product(s) they are emulating. On the other hand, products that are major advances to existing competition, or even breakthrough items, are more difficult for customers to place a monetary value on and therefore face more challenges in product pricing.

Managers of products that are directly comparable to existing products must be cognizant of the existing price-value perceptions in the market. Deviating too far from what customers currently view as acceptable requires care. A product priced substantially below the competition could trigger skepticism of its quality unless there are clear signals of the appropriate value. On the other hand, a product priced significantly higher could generate a negative reaction unless the competitive superiority is clearly visible. Since customers will use the price of existing alternatives as the reference point to judge fairness of the new product price, the product manager must do so as well. From this reference point the product manager must add or subtract the estimated monetary value (to the customers) of product features and attributes that are different from the existing product.

The pricing of completely new products cannot start with a competitive reference point as in the case with line extension products. This can make customer research more difficult, but there is also a benefit in that customer perceptions are not restricted by current competitive prices. Nevertheless, it's useful to start the pricing analysis with a reference price. This can be the price of the closest possible alternative or substitute for the new product or service, or it can be the cost of providing the same functionality that the new product or service provides.

The process of estimating the price of most new products starts with expert opinions. This is especially true for breakthrough and business-to-business products. Individuals with knowledge of the industry—sales, marketing, general management, key stakeholders—are asked to provide their best price-volume estimates. The estimates are revised (in a group meeting or through a Delphi process) until consensus is reached. The resulting information may be augmented by

(**Reflection Point**)

What types of new products do I
generally launch?

- What experts (in or out of the
  company) could shed light on
  appropriate prices?

- What reference prices do customers
  use to judge the fairness of the new
  product price?
- What information do customers
  generally have at their disposal when
  making a purchase decision for this
  type of product?

market studies, experiments, and/or analysis of historical price data of analogous
products.[2]

Customers are not always reliable sources for new product pricing information. Nevertheless, surveys can provide some useful information, especially
for industrial products where customers make deliberate purchase decisions.
Instead of asking customers what price they would be willing to pay for a new
product, it is usually better to provide different prices and ask them their likelihood to buy at each price. To accomplish this, provide customers with the competitive performance and price data they would likely have at their disposal if
they were making a purchase decision. Honestly explain the differential benefits
of the new product and provide perhaps three price points. Then provide a five-
or seven-point scale anchored with "definitely would buy" and "definitely would
not buy."

Pricing Product Line Extensions

Product managers must frequently bring out additions to a product line that may
include replacements, product variants, and complementary items. Although
these are new products, as discussed in the previous section, the strategy for

---

2. For more detail on pricing research, refer to Robert J. Dolan and Hermann Simon, *Power Pricing*
   (New York: The Free Press, 1996). Chapter 3 on price estimation response includes a good
   discussion of new product pricing.

pricing them is linked to the strategy of other products in the line. Replacement products are substitutes for current offerings. Variants are those targeted at particular niches (e.g., price-sensitive segments) or specific applications. Complementary items are those intended for use with existing products. In any of these situations, the price of one product may affect the sales of another, so it's important to think about the product *line* impacts and contribution margins when establishing base prices.

The price of a replacement may not be as major an issue if the timing of the new product launch exactly matches the sale of the last product it replaces. In reality product rollovers are rarely that precise, and a wrong price could result in the old product becoming obsolete in inventory or the new product success being damaged by slow initial sales. Therefore, it's important to think about the prices of both the existing and substitute products simultaneously and build that into the launch plan. Several strategies may be appropriate.

1. Price the new product high, encouraging price-sensitive customers to buy the old product, with innovators choosing the new product. When pipeline inventory is depleted, the replacement product can be repriced, if necessary.
2. Sell the products through different channels responding to different price points.
3. Drastically reduce the price of the old product to get it out of inventory.
4. Make the determination of which strategy to use by computing the overall contribution of the combined products.

Product variants are generally intended *not* to be viewed as substitutes. For example, products of a different size, shape, or feature set may fit specific applications but not others. There may be different values associated with the different applications and that could likely affect the appropriate price to charge. Similarly, products may be deliberately de-featured to justify a lower price for a product targeted at a price-sensitive group of customers. Product managers must distinguish the variants by selling them through different channels, making the products and packaging visually different, using different brand names, and using other techniques to justify price differentials.

Some product variants are intended to be part of a competitive strategy, most commonly against an aggressive price competitor. Rather than cut prices directly, the "fighting brand" is intended to offer the customer another alternative. Typically priced between the existing product's price and the competitor's price, the fighting brand strives to draw most sales from the competitor (although there will be some sales shifted from the existing product). Another

---

How does the pricing strategy for line extensions incorporate other products in the line?

• What pricing variants are appropriate for "fighting brands," entry-level offerings, and other product alternatives?

• How should add-on features be priced?
• Should complementary products be bundled together for a single price?

---

alternative may be to offer additional features on the product and sell it at the same price, since customers often accept extras in lieu of price concessions.

Other product variants are intended to be entry-level or premium extensions. Entry-level products are used to attract new customers to the firm, with the goal of having them remain loyal and trade up in the future. Premium extensions are used to offer existing customers a better alternative. In either of these cases, product managers must determine whether a different brand is necessary to maintain the clear quality differences between the offerings.

Complementary products are those that augment the sales of a source product—for example, razor blades are complements to razors. The objective when there are both source and complementary products is to price the *combination* in a manner that increases profit from the whole line. Many companies choose to attain a lower margin on the source product (e.g., a piece of equipment) to ensure future sales of a higher-margin complementary product (e.g., consumables). This can be a challenge if each product is expected to carry its weight in terms of contribution, or if the products are under the responsibility of different product managers.

Price Decision Factors

There are several other factors that could influence the appropriate price a product manager should charge for a product or service, such as stage of the product lifecycle, values associated with having the products available at different times and locations (i.e., time and place utility), and expected marketplace reactions.

The traditional product lifecycle moves from introduction through growth and maturity to decline. The price of a new product, as mentioned earlier, depends partly on how innovative it is. An innovative product that is unlikely to be quickly copied by the competition can support a high price (i.e., a skimming policy), whereas a product that will be quickly copied will not have the same latitude. In either case the price should be high enough to allow decreases as competition enters the market. As products move through growth and maturity, the amount of price protection they have depends on the perceived differentiation they have in the marketplace. During the decline phase, product managers must decide whether to have "fire-sale" prices to get the product out of inventory, or to price high to encourage customers to shift to newer substitute products.

Where and when products are sold can also influence price sensitivity. A hot dog sold at a ballpark will cost substantially more than the same item sold at a supermarket, due to the convenience and experience of the purchase. Conference and airline pricing can vary according to the amount of time prior to the service that the purchase was made.

Think about the market expectations in your industry. Does your market expect steadily decreasing prices (or consistent improvements for the same price)? Then use this information to make pricing decisions.

Pricing Supplementary Services and Options

Many products are bundled with supplementary services and options. These could include technical problem solving, training, equipment installation, maintenance, customer product design, logistics management, and a host of other

---

Reflection Point

How do I determine prices for supplementary services and options?

- What customers would rather pay for services than lose them? How much would they be willing to pay?

- Do I "throw in" services to get a product sale without giving any thought to the value?

---

services. Similar to the main product, these services and options might not be valued the same by all customers. Yet product managers generally focus on the product and largely ignore tailoring services. They might be providing customers with more services than they want or need at prices that often reflect neither their value nor their cost.

While it is true that some services may need to be "thrown in" to get specific product sales, this is often done routinely without any thought to whether it is necessary or appropriate. Which customers truly value the services and would rather pay for them than not have them at all? What price would be acceptable to these customers? Could you modify product prices by charging for services? Could you charge differential prices for services based on the value assessed by different customer segments?

Price Erosion in the Industry

Price declines can occur in an industry due to many factors: changes in technology, increased competition, customer consolidation, or commodity perceptions related to a mature industry. Dealing with the price erosion should start with identifying and responding to the factor(s) that caused it. Otherwise, unfounded price-cutting can precipitate a price war that is troublesome for all companies in the industry. Some tactics for dealing with price erosion include:

- segment the market based on price sensitivity and target those less price sensitive (or offer a good-better-best product line)
- develop exclusive channels to protect premium price/brand loyalty

• create marketing communications to demonstrate unique product differences and/or to prove the lifetime value of the purchase
• repackage the product to reinforce its worth
• eliminate features that cost more than the benefit to customers
• establish long-term contracts (specifying quality, customization, etc.) with customers to reduce their migration to competition for a lower price
• establish cumulative reward offerings (loyalty programs)
• identify new markets or applications for the product
• encourage customers to upgrade to higher-margin products

Initiating Price Changes

Product managers often hesitate to raise prices for fear of losing business. Yet price increases are often a necessity. Some tactics to help in initiating price increases include:

• time the price increase with added value (e.g., service or product change)
• bundle additional services with the main product
• co-brand or co-market with another company to establish a differentiated position
• show the long-term value of a future trade-in
• differentiate the company, not just the product

Price decreases are easier to implement, but they may still carry a few risks. A price decrease may cause customers to wonder whether there has been a decline in quality, or worst yet, whether you have been "gouging" them in the past. Therefore, price declines must be administered carefully.

Reflection Point

What steps would make price changes easier?

- What services or features could be added, deleted, or changed with minimal expense?

- How can I position the price change from a customer perspective?

Sales Force Discounting

Price concessions can have a major impact on profitability. A study by McKinsey discovered that for the average Standard & Poor's 1000 company, a 1 percent price change (all else being the same) equated with an approximate 12 percent change in the bottom line.[3] In fact, for a specific percentage, a change in price will impact profitability more than for the same percentage change in volume, variable costs, or fixed costs. Although the percentage profit impacts will vary by differences in income statements, the *relative* differences will reflect what is shown as follows:

	ORIGINAL	1% PRICE INCREASE	1% VOLUME INCREASE	1% CUT IN CGS	1% CUT IN FIXED COSTS
Sales (5,000 × $200)	$1,000,000	$1,010,000	$1,010,000	$1,000,000	$1,000,000
CGS (5,000 × $110)	550,000	550,000	555,500	544,500	550,000
Gross margin	450,000	460,000	454,500	455,500	450,000
Operating costs	350,000	350,000	350,000	350,000	346,500
Net pretax income	$100,000	$110,000	$104,500	$105,500	$103,500
% change in income		10%	4.5%	5.5%	3.5%

3. Sarah Lorge, "The Crisis with Prices," *Sales and Marketing Management,* August 1997, p. 26.

In many companies, salespeople are given significant latitude in discounting prices to attain a sale. Some firms provide a discount range or price floor below which they need to get product manager approval before offering the price to a customer. Beyond establishing these types of discount policies some tactics for reducing the potential problem of excessive discounting include the following:

• Educate the sales force on the financial impact of discounting (using the type of information presented earlier in the comparative table).
• Establish quota and incentive programs for the sales force based on price realization or margin.
• Provide sales collateral and training focused on overcoming the price objection.

Global Pricing

As product managers increasingly sell products beyond the domestic borders, or as more of their customers become global, the question of how to price becomes more complex. While there are no easy answers to the question, there are factors that suggest when prices should be customized for specific markets, as well as factors that suggest when prices should be as globally harmonized as possible. Where the competition, customer expectations, and costs vary dramatically by regions, differential prices may be necessary. Similarly, differing exchange rates, duties, and customs may necessitate various surcharges. On the other hand, free trade agreements, and "efficient" distribution channels and communication

> ### Reflection Point
>
> What have I done to improve the pricing of global products?
>
> • What factors suggest that I should customize the prices by market?
>
> • What factors suggest that I should offer one price (or a limited price range)?
>
> • Which factors are strongest?

networks (e.g., the Internet) may result in customers demanding common prices. These forces must be weighed carefully to decide on the best approach to global pricing. Product managers are encouraged to refer to *Power Pricing* by Robert J. Dolan and Hermann Simon (primarily Chapter 6) for a more thorough discussion of global pricing.[4]

KEY POINTS
- Relate the pricing of your product line to the "umbrella" pricing strategy of your company.
- Determine the reference prices customers use to judge the fairness of new products prices.
- Price products in conjunction with related products in the line.
- Evaluate the value of supplementary services to determine whether they should be priced rather than given away free.
- Avoid price wars by using creative means of dealing with price erosion.
- Plan price changes along with relevant product changes.
- Establish boundaries for sales force discounting.
- Balance customization and harmonization factors when deciding on global prices.

---

4. Robert J. Dolan and Hermann Simon, *Power Pricing* (New York: The Free Press, 1996), Chapter 6.

PRICING CHECKLIST

PRICING GOALS AND OBJECTIVES

Have you identified your corporate price position or strategy?	Yes	No
Do you address the three Cs in price evaluations?	Yes	No
Do you have true cost information to aid in decision making?	Yes	No
Do you have data on customer price sensitivity?	Yes	No
Do you have data on competitive price positioning?	Yes	No

NEW PRODUCT PRICING

Have you determined the competitive reference points customers use to evaluate new product prices?	Yes	No
Can you use the historical price data of analogous products to estimate future price trends of new products?	Yes	No

PRICING PRODUCT LINE EXTENSIONS

Have you categorized line items as replacements, product variants, or complements?	Yes	No
Do you simultaneously evaluate prices of existing and replacement products as part of the launch plan?	Yes	No
Do you alter the marketing program for product variants to clearly distinguish them from other products in the line?	Yes	No
Do you price the combination of source and complementary products in a way that increases overall profit?	Yes	No

PRICE DECISION FACTORS

Is product lifecycle stage considered in pricing?	Yes	No
Do you determine the value of time and place utility, and build that into your prices?	Yes	No

PRICING CHECKLIST, *continued*

PRICING SUPPLEMENTARY SERVICES AND OPTIONS

Do you know whether customers would rather pay for services
than lose them?   Yes   No

Have you estimated how much customers would be willing
to pay?   Yes   No

PRICE EROSION IN THE INDUSTRY

Have you explored all options to avoid a price war?   Yes   No

Do you test creative marketing tactics prior to cutting price? Yes   No

INITIATING PRICE CHANGES

Do you plan product and service changes to coincide with
price changes?   Yes   No

Do customers prefer advance notification of price changes? Yes   No

SALES FORCE DISCOUNTING

Does your sales force really know the financial impact of
discounting?   Yes   No

Have you provided training and support material to help them
overcome price objections?   Yes   No

GLOBAL PRICING

Do customer and market conditions favor regional pricing? Yes   No

Do customer and market conditions favor one global price? Yes   No

11

Integrated Marketing Communications

"The only place that real product or brand value exists is within the minds of the customers or prospects. All the other marketing variables, such as product design, pricing, distribution, and availability, can be copied, duplicated, or overcome by competitors. What exists in the mental network of the [customer] or the prospect is truly where marketing value resides."

> —Don E. Schultz, Stanley I. Tannenbaum, Robert F. Lauterborn, coauthors, *Integrated Marketing Communications: Pulling It Together and Making It Work*[1]

The key purpose of marketing communications is to communicate to customers the value created by an overall marketing program, as well as to contribute to the program's effectiveness. This is accomplished by changing attitudes, increasing sales, or establishing a price-value proposition. Product managers' role responsibilities with regard to these issues vary by company. Although some are expected to write copy and work with the media, others leave these tasks to advertising agencies and internal communications departments. Regardless of the level of direct involvement, a product manager should be the *integrator* of all communications related to his or her products and services. Product managers must understand the brand equity and positioning of the products and services in their area of responsibility, coordinate the communications tasks necessary to solve a specific problem, and be able to critique the relevant promotional plans and activities.

---

1. Don E. Schultz, Stanley I. Tannenbaum, and Robert F. Lauterborn, *Integrated Marketing Communications: Pulling It Together and Making It Work* (New York: McGraw-Hill, 1993) p. 45.

FIGURE 11.1 *The Four Cs of Communications*

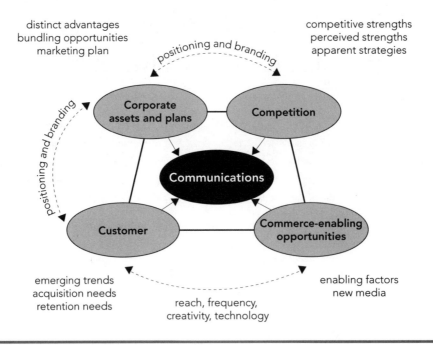

Marketing Communications

Figure 11.1 shows the four Cs surrounding marketing communications: corporate assets and plans, competition, customer, and commerce-enabling opportunities. *Corporate assets* refer to the internal strengths, assets, and skills that provide the foundation for a strong offering to the market. What features and benefits does your product offer? What additional services and relationships can be built on company strengths? (Refer to Chapter 6 for a discussion of the total solution product.) The marketing plan is another internal consideration in determining direction for a marketing communications program. Next, analyze your strengths in conjunction with the strengths and apparent strategies of the *competition* to look for openings to position your product or brand as "better than the competition." Of course, while doing so, always keep the *customer* viewpoint in mind. Even if you find an aspect of your offering that is better than the competition, you must always ask yourself whether anyone cares. As part of the C of customer, determine the acquisition and retention goals that may be part of your overall marketing plan. Finally examine external means of reaching your audience—that is, *commerce-enabling opportunities*. Are there new trade shows, events, or mail lists to pursue? Have you utilized electronic media to your benefit? Do you have the appropriate reach, frequency, and creativity so that your media expenditures are not wasted?

When companies refer to "marketing" their products, they generally mean either selling (the output of the sales force) or advertising (the output of marketing communications). Product managers are involved with both these aspects of marketing, as well as the full range of marketing and marketing communications. The product and related services must be integrated with the pricing and distribution strategy and with all communication messages. Therefore, product managers are most likely expected to develop: (a) concise, articulate descriptions of the product's positioning (brand equity), target customer profile, and key benefits; (b) strategies for integrating communications into the product's marketing plan to achieve stated objectives; and (c) sales support materials such as spec sheets for products and capabilities sheets for services. Product managers might also be involved in other complementary communications efforts such as trade shows, sales presentations, and public relations events.

Brand Equity and Positioning

A strong brand is the mental "executive summary" of what the company or product stands for in the customer's mind. It is . . .

- part of a strategy of differentiation and segmentation (as mentioned in Chapter 6, Toyota and Lexus have differentiated identities and appeal to different market segments)
- built on realities of organizational culture, assets, human resources, and values
- the implicit promise to or contract of performance with the customer(s)

A brand is an implicit, deliverable promise to your customers. The promise could be one of customer service, unique product features, top quality, low price, emotions such as fun and excitement, or any other benefit. How much the target customers value these factors is your brand equity. This level of brand equity can

FIGURE 11.2 *Components of Brand Development*

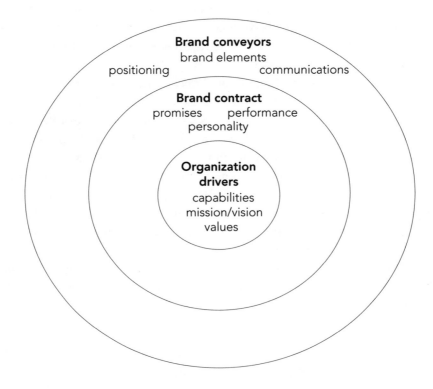

Source: Adapted from F. Joseph LePla and Lynn M. Parker, *Integrated Branding* (Westport, CT: Quorum Books, 1999) p. 15.

only be built on trust. The positioning refers to how the customer perceives this value compared to something else, for example, the competition or other products in your line, as a component of a total solution. Ask yourself the following questions:

- What is your product identity (your brand)?
- What value (brand equity) does this identity have for customers?
- How do target customers perceive this brand compared to the competition (your positioning)?
- Is the customer perception what you want it to be, and is it consistent with your goals?

Before product managers can claim a specific brand position, they must determine whether the promises they make are truly deliverable to the customer. This means that the brand has to be consistent with the capabilities of the firm, as well as its mission, vision, and values. These are the *organization drivers* behind the brand, as shown in the inner ring of Figure 11.2. For example, if part of the brand identity is superior customer service, the firm must have enough trained and motivated customer service representatives to provide this level of service. If the brand identity is one of innovation, there must be a culture of innovation in the firm and supported R&D function.

After clarifying the organization drivers, the next level of brand development is to define the *brand contract* (middle ring). Determine what your customers believe you have promised (e.g., fast turnaround) and translate that into standards of performance (e.g., all orders shipped within 48 hours). Also, think about the nuances of your brand personality. Is your brand fun? Exciting? Dependable? Conservative? Volvo, for instance, is associated with safety and therefore has a more conservative personality.

Next you must *convey* your brand (its promises, performance, and personality) to customers—the outer ring in Figure 11.2. When Milk Chug® was launched to appeal to the youth market, Dean Foods realized it would need to compete against soft drinks and other beverages to be successful. Therefore, it created unique packaging (a resealable plastic bottle in the shape of an old milk jug) in various sizes and introduced a variety of flavors. The brand name and packaging conveyed the "fun" personality, and the product itself (milk) promised a healthy alternative to the competitors (the beverage market). Let's write a positioning statement for this brand. The statement should specify the competitors or alternatives the market would consider in buying the product (i.e., the competitive frame of reference), the specific point of differentiation between the offering and the competition, and the features, services, or other competencies that prove the firm can deliver on the differentiating value promised to customers. This knowledge helps in writing and evaluating any future marketing communication messages. The positioning statement for Milk Chug® might be:

To <u>the youth market,</u> <u>Milk Chug®</u> is the brand of <u>beverage</u>
defined target market *brand name* *competitive frame*
of reference

that is <u>nutritious and fun</u> due to <u>content plus creative packaging.</u>
point of differentiation *distinctive competence*

FIGURE 11.3 *Brand Communications Checklist*

THE BRAND COMMUNICATIONS . . .	YES	NO
talk to specific target customers, internally and externally		
clearly differentiate the brand(s) from the competition		
reinforce positive customer experiences		
are integrated and coherent across all relevant media		
have both emotional and rational components		
are consistent throughout the value chain		
articulate a memorable and compelling brand promise		
establish trust and credibility for the brand promise		
incorporate co-branding efforts where appropriate		
balance consistency and flexibility		

Next, evaluate your brand elements. Brand elements include (but are not limited to) trademarkable aspects such as:

- brand name
- logos
- symbols
- characters
- slogans
- jingles
- packages
- sound

Are these brand elements memorable, meaningful (e.g., descriptive of the promise), transferable (across media and markets), flexible, and/or able to be protected (perhaps through legal means)?[2]

---

2. Refer to Kevin Lane Keller, *Strategic Brand Management: Building, Measuring, and Managing Brand Equity* (New York: Prentice Hall, 1998) for a good discussion of using brand elements to build brand equity.

Now you are ready to integrate your brand building efforts into your marketing communications program. A firm must be very careful when its marketing communications go against a previously strong identity. Coca-Cola, for example, tried to boost sales of its flagship brand by developing an "edgy" campaign a few years ago. Rather than the traditional "warm and fuzzy" ads, the new campaign featured a commercial with a crotchety grandmother who went ballistic when Coca-Cola was not present at a family reunion. Another commercial showed two high school friends fighting when there was no Coke at their graduation. Consumers and bottlers complained that the advertising was "mean-spirited," and the campaign was quickly pulled.[3] The brand identity should be consistent throughout your sales channel and across all of your customer contacts, from corporate stationery to advertising to E-mails. Use the checklist in Figure 11.3 to appraise your brand communications.

Integrating the Marketing Communications

As mentioned earlier, a key purpose of marketing communications is to communicate to customers the value created by the overall marketing program, as well as to contribute to its effectiveness. For the product manager, this implies several things. First, the product manager must decide on the general direction necessary

---

3. Betsy McKay and Suzanne Vranica, "How a Coke Ad Campaign Fell Flat with Viewers," *The Wall Street Journal*, March 19, 2001, p. B1+.

for the marketing communications program to accomplish the product's marketing plan objectives. Once the plan is in place, the product manager will need to work with the department or agency developing the promotional pieces and monitor the effectiveness of the program. Their involvement in creating a marketing communications program includes the following:

1. Determine what must happen to attain marketing plan goals.
2. Restate in quantitative terms.
3. Carefully define the target customer(s).
4. Think like a customer.
5. Establish a creative platform.
6. Develop an integrated media strategy and schedule.
7. Set objectives for media and tactics.
8. Establish an acceptable budget.
9. Work with the agency or staff to execute the plan.
10. Evaluate results.

Determine What Must Happen to Attain Marketing Plan Goals

The starting point is to refer back to the objectives as specified in the marketing plan (see the discussion of goals and objectives in Chapter 3). Is your umbrella marketing objective, for example, to increase the sales of bundled products to select markets? If so, what communications efforts would help achieve that objective? What is the profile of each of the select markets? Will you reach the end user directly (pull strategy) or indirectly through the channel (push strategy)? What is the competitive advantage of the product bundle compared to individual purchases and to competitor offerings? Are you attempting to create awareness, preference, or purchase through your communications program? Is your goal to get prospects to try the bundled product (so as to increase the probability of future purchases)?

Restate in Quantitative Terms

Once you have decided what you would like to happen, you will need to restate that goal in quantitative (measurable) terms, such as, "obtain trial by 25 percent of identified prospects during the first quarter."

Define Target Customer(s)

Use both psychographic and demographic terms to define your target customers. The *psychographic description* (e.g., attitudes, opinions, lifestyle) aids in writing the message. The *demographic description* (NAICS, title, geography, age, income) aids in media selection. Sometimes there are different target audiences for a product that require subtly different messages or media. For example, a contractor may have one need for a garage door (e.g., to complete a job), a home-owner may have a different need (e.g., ease of installation), and an architect may have still another need (e.g., aesthetic fit with a building design). In addition, for many products, especially business products, the user may be different from the purchaser or other influencers, and each may have different reasons for wanting a particular product. The product manager must determine which groups are most important for accomplishing the overall objectives, and whether separate communications strategies are necessary for different audiences.

Think Like a Customer

Thinking like a target customer really requires projecting yourself into his or her shoes. Why might customers want this product at this time? How do they feel about the purchase? What objections might they have, and does your product pose any risk to them? What alternatives might they be considering? Does your product fit their need or application precisely? Where do your customers look for advice on making the purchase? Why should customers believe your product is better than the competition in satisfying their needs? How are customers buying the product (or getting their needs addressed) now? Remember what it is that customers want to know:

- What will your product (service) do for me?
- How will it do this?
- Why is it better than the competition?
- Who says so?
- What if I'm not satisfied?

Establish a Creative Platform

Once you understand your defined target customer perceptions, the information can be used to write a creative platform for the product or service. Be prepared to put some objectivity into the creative process by carefully addressing some important questions.

- Who—specifically—are you trying to reach?
- What is the main point of the message you want to communicate?
- Why should they care?
- Why should they believe you? Is the competitive advantage clear?
- What should they do or feel as a result of the communication?

CREATIVE PLATFORM

Market profile	Describe the "person" you are talking to.
Main point of message	What is the one-word, *big* idea?
Intended impact on audience	What should the person *feel* and *do*, and why should that person *care*?
Proof statement	Provide reasons for the person to believe you.

Develop an Integrated Media Schedule

The next step is to determine how to communicate this positioning to your customers. Which media and media vehicles (1) have audience profiles that best match your target market demographics and (2) minimize contacts that are not in your target market? What percent of your customers can you reach using these media (i.e., what is the *reach* of the program)? How frequently will you need to reach customers to accomplish your goals (i.e., what is the *frequency*)? Would it be better for your product to be consistently in the customer's mind (i.e., *continuity*) or could you better spend your resources by grouping your messages into a smaller time frame to get a stronger short-term impact on the market (i.e., *flighting*)? For example, if your budget allows you to advertise twice a month and you don't feel that would have sufficient impact, you could choose to group your ads (perhaps four every two months) into a flighting campaign for more impact. Plotting each of these contacts on a calendar will help you visualize the frequency and/or continuity of your approach. Be thorough in looking at potential customer contact points so that you don't miss emerging media or nontraditional customer contacts. For example, if the goal is to encourage prospects to try a product, you might consider the following:

- Alter your channel strategy to be present where prospects buy.
- Establish a direct mail campaign to notify them of the new channel (or of your website if they can buy direct).
- Advertise in targeted media.
- Attend a new trade show directed at this particular market segment.
- Modify packaging to appeal to the prospects.
- Develop a contest to encourage trial.
- Arrange an open house where the product can be sampled.
- Provide samples to associations to share with their members.
- Send out press releases announcing the new product, the ability to send for a free (or low-cost) sample, and so forth.

Set Objectives for Media and Tactics

In addition to the overall communications objective, it is often useful to set sub-objectives for specific media or tactics. For example, if you use direct response as part of your communications effort, you might set objectives for specific response rates or leads generated. For events, you might set objectives for new customers contacted and names added to the database. For publicity, you might set objectives for the number of press releases published. For contests, you might set objectives for short-term sales increases.

Establish a Budget

Marketing communications budgets are determined in many ways. Many companies use a percentage of anticipated sales as a target. This percentage varies significantly by industry. Each year, *Advertising Age* magazine publishes advertising expenditures for leading national advertisers, including an estimate of U.S. revenue per ad dollar. By inverting this ratio (i.e., ad dollar divided by revenue figure), you obtain an estimate of the advertising as a percent of sales. For example, in 2001 the range of revenue per ad dollar was $3.70 (for L'Oréal and Estée Lauder) to $318.00 (for Wal-Mart). The approximate percent of sales, therefore, ranged from 27 percent to less than 1 percent. Looking at the percent of sales spent on advertising for a firm in a related industry provides one more data point in determining the appropriate figure to use for your budget.

Product managers should also attempt to budget using the *objective-and-task* method. With this method, the product manager determines what it would take to achieve the stated objectives for the marketing communications plan, and then estimates the cost of the related tasks and activities. For example, if past history suggests that 2 percent of customers buy your product as a result of a direct mail campaign, and your goal is to sell 500 units, you would need to mail out 25,000 direct mail pieces. The cost of the printing, postage, labor, and so forth would therefore be the budget for the program. If your objective is to generate 300 qualified leads for the sales force, and history suggests that it takes a minimum of three contacts per prospect to attain the leads, you would need to estimate the reach, frequency, and appropriate cost to accomplish this objective. If your objective is to generate specific dollar sales revenue, you will need to determine what the average sales revenue is per lead, and then determine the number of leads necessary to generate this total revenue.

Execute the Plan

Now that the plan is in place, the product manager is responsible for working with the internal department or advertising agency to put the plan into action. In most cases, this involves monitoring progress and quality of a communications program. In appraising the creative work of others (or even yourself), refer back to the creative platform to ensure that the planning issues have been addressed. Then add a few more questions:

- Is there a promise to or benefit for the customer?
- Does it pass the "so what?" test?
- Is it relevant and believable to the target market?
  For how long?
- Is it consistent (integrated) with the other communications?
- Is it consistent with the desired brand equity and positioning?

  In appraising the media plan, ask the following:

- How many potential viewers of the message exist?
- How often must they see the message for it to have an impact?
- What are the advantages and disadvantages of the various media relative to your message, market, and objectives?
- Have you attained the best reach and frequency within budget?

Evaluate Results

Finally, during and after the marketing communication campaign, evaluate the process. On a micro basis, evaluate whether the individual communication tools

> ## Reflection Point
>
> How well do I plan for and monitor an integrated marketing communications campaign?
>
> - What improvements can I make in setting objectives?
>
> - Do I prepare useful creative platforms and target audience profiles?
> - What measures can I incorporate into the plan to monitor progress?

achieved their objectives. Did you generate the expected number of inquiries or leads from the direct mail program? Did you have the expected number of people at the open house? Did you get an acceptable percentage of press releases published? Did you achieve the desired readership in the trade journal? Did you get the estimated registration on your website? In addition to these micro evaluations, you should also evaluate whether the entire campaign helped you accomplish the overall (macro) communications objectives.

Sales Support Materials

Product managers are frequently involved in developing and providing collateral materials for the sales force. (Collateral material for the sales channel is discussed in Chapter 12.) This requires that product managers understand the sales process and how salespeople are likely to use the materials to "advance the sales call." The traditional sales process includes:

- planning
- establishing trust
- qualifying needs
- persuading prospect of solution

Product managers can help salespeople in the planning phase by identifying the best target market for their products, providing strong leads, and describing the target market in both psychographic and demographic terms. Trust can be enhanced by providing print materials that establish credibility and communicate a strong brand identity. Trust can also be enhanced by corporate advertising and

Reflection Point

How can I make my collateral materials "advance the sales effort" of the sales force?

- How can I assist the sales force in each step of the sales process?
- What improvements can I make in my communications with the sales force?

public relations activities. Product managers can assist salespeople in qualifying prospects by suggesting solid questions that differentiate between customers who "fit" and those that don't. Persuading customers that your product is the best solution for their problems may require convincing buyers, users, and influencers—which may entail different types of collateral materials.

Complementary Communications Efforts

There are several events that might complement the communications efforts of a product manager. A sampling of some events might include:

- open houses
- plant tours
- technical seminars
- news conferences
- cause-related telethons
- celebrity appearances
- remote broadcasts
- ground-breaking ceremonies
- sporting events
- concerts
- lectures
- contests
- festivals
- award presentations

Reflection Point

What events might I try to augment my marketing communications efforts?

- Is there something that I haven't tried before but has worked in other industries?
- Are there ways I can share the cost of the event with other businesses?

As you are planning events, ask yourself how well they support your integrated communications efforts. Ensure that they enhance, strengthen, or maintain the brand equity for your product and your company. Some considerations in leveraging your budget include the following:[4]

- piggybacking on an already established event
- finding cosponsors
- sharing the costs with a firm offering a complementary product or service

KEY POINTS
- Define your brand identity, brand equity, and positioning prior to starting a marketing communications campaign.
- Determine whether the customer perception of you is what you want it to be, or if you need to work toward changing it.
- Write a positioning statement that clarifies what your competitive differentiation is, and why it is "real."
- Follow the 10-step process of integrating marketing communications.
- Develop sales collateral that helps salespeople "advance the sales call."
- Creatively explore public relations activities and events that may contribute to your communications efforts.

---

4. See Roman G. Hiebing, Jr., and Scott W. Cooper, *How to Write a Successful Marketing Plan*, 2e (Chicago: NTC Business Books, 1997) for more tips on establishing promotional objectives and plans.

MARKETING COMMUNICATIONS CHECKLIST

BRAND EQUITY AND POSITIONING

Have you defined your brand identity?	Yes	No
Have you determined the value (brand equity) this identity has for customers?	Yes	No
Do your brand communications clearly differentiate the brand from the competition?	Yes	No
Do your brand communications articulate a memorable and compelling brand promise?	Yes	No
Are your brand communications integrated with other marketing communication efforts?	Yes	No

INTEGRATING THE MARKETING COMMUNICATIONS

Have you determined what must happen to attain your marketing goals?	Yes	No
Did you restate this in quantitative terms?	Yes	No
Have you profiled the target customer in both psychographic and demographic terms?	Yes	No
Do you know what customers want from your product?	Yes	No
Have you established a creative platform?	Yes	No
Does your media schedule provide the reach, frequency, and continuity necessary to accomplish your goals?	Yes	No
Have you established a relevant budget?	Yes	No
Do you maintain control over the execution phase of the program?	Yes	No
Have you determined what measures to use to evaluate results?	Yes	No

MARKETING COMMUNICATIONS CHECKLIST, *continued*

SALES SUPPORT MATERIALS

Have you developed your sales collateral materials with an
understanding of a typical sales call by your salespeople?   Yes   No

Do you build in flexibility for salespeople to adapt your materials
as necessary?   Yes   No

COMPLEMENTARY COMMUNICATIONS EFFORTS

Do you incorporate public relations activities and events into
your planning?   Yes   No

Are these events consistent with your marketing communications
and brand messages?   Yes   No

Do you look for ways to share the cost of these activities?   Yes   No

12

"Go to Market" Strategies

"If you haven't looked closely, a major trend could have slipped by. A combination of technological, demographic, and competitive forces have changed the market your distributors face. New channels have grabbed a higher share of market, and the remaining market for traditional wholesale distributors has changed, too."

—Neil Gillespie, principal of the
Channel Marketing Group[1]

For products or services to be successful in the marketplace, they must be available where customers want to buy them and how customers want to use them. These approaches are called *go to market strategies*. Banks have opened branches in grocery stores and now provide phone and Internet account accessibility. Some industrial firms have augmented their traditional channels with "big box" retailers to either reach new customers or offer existing customers more options. Other fundamental marketing changes that may affect go to market approaches include the following:[2]

- increasing emphasis on key account and customer segment managers
- assignment of teams to major accounts
- stronger strategic orientation in product management
- organizational systems aligned to focus on customers

---

1. From the website of Channel Marketing Group, channelmkt.com.

2. Christian Homburg, John Workman, and Ove Jensen, "Fundamental Changes in Marketing Organization: The Movement Toward a Customer-Focused Organizational Structure," *Academy of Marketing Science Journal,* Fall 2000, pp. 459–478.

FIGURE 12.1 *Range of Distribution Issues*

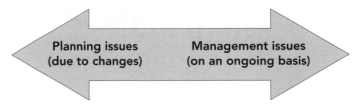

Planning issues (due to changes)	Management issues (on an ongoing basis)

- Should we change the way we go to market?
- Should we change, add, or delete individual intermediaries?
- Should we reallocate functions between the manufacturer and members?
- Should we change distributor contracts?

- How can we motivate the channel to sell more?
- How can we better align our marketing objectives with our channel objectives?
- How can we improve communications within the channel?
- How can we increase channel effectiveness?

Although these strategic changes are beyond the product manager's sole responsibility, he or she should have input into the decisions. In addition, the product manager helps provide ongoing support to the channel, for example, in terms of product literature. The range of decisions is shown in Figure 12.1.

Product managers are generally not integrators of distribution channels the way they are integrators of marketing communications, but they nevertheless carry a responsibility for their effectiveness. They must work with salespeople or resellers to implement the marketing plans for their products. This chapter looks at some of the questions of strategic fit and tactical support necessary for improved effectiveness.

Strategic Fit Questions

Dell Computer Corporation is a company that has long focused on a direct channel to reach its customers; it was a leader in direct sales by telephone and the Internet. Then it added kiosks in shopping malls as another way to reach consumers. Next, the growth of "white-box PCs" (no-name computers put together from parts of various suppliers) to small businesses through dealers spurred the company to evaluate this channel as well. Since many small businesses essentially view the local dealers as their information technology (IT) department, they are less inclined to purchase direct. They value the training, installation, and repair services they get from the dealer, as well as the face-to-face contact. To reach this group of customers, Dell began offering an unbranded PC to U.S. dealers.[3]

Many other firms have made strategic channel changes. Avon decided to augment its direct consumer sales channel.[4] Since the average age of the customers in its traditional channel was slowly increasing, it decided to open boutiques in J. C. Penney stores to reach a younger, working market. Avon's new retail line will target women 25–29, instead of its typical customer, whose age is 40–55. Similarly, many industrial companies have augmented their traditional direct or distributor sales channels with Internet ordering for specific products or customers.

A channel refers to the various "selling contact points" between the company and its end customers, as shown in the four examples of Figure 12.2. There may be a variety of direct sales channels (reaching customers through a direct sales force, telesales, direct mail, the Internet, company-owned stores, etc.) and indirect sales channels (reaching customers through independent reps, distributors, dealers, retailers, etc.). Draw your own channel; understanding the existing structures and performance is the first step in improving their effectiveness.

When there is a direct sales force, as in the case of many companies with business-to-business (B2B) products or services, product managers will likely be involved with product training and motivating the sales force to sell specific products or systems to the appropriate customers. If direct mail or the Internet is used, product managers may write (or approve) the selling message to customers. When using the Internet, product managers should decide on the appropriate objectives, as shown in Figure 12.3.

Product managers may also work with indirect channels. Manufacturer (or independent) reps are individuals or agencies that function as an external sales force for a firm. Sometimes called brokers or agents, these organizations bring together the buyer and seller, generally do not take title, and are paid through commissions. Most industrial reps carry noncompeting products from many firms, but this is not as true for consumer reps. Distributors (and wholesalers)

---

3. Gary McWilliams, "In About-Face, Dell Will Sell PCs to Dealers," *The Wall Street Journal*, August 20, 2002, p. B1.

4. Alicia Zappier, "Avon to Unveil New Cosmetics Line at Sears, Penney Beauty Centers," *Drug Store News*, October 30, 2000, p. 39.

FIGURE 12.2 *Example Distribution Channels*

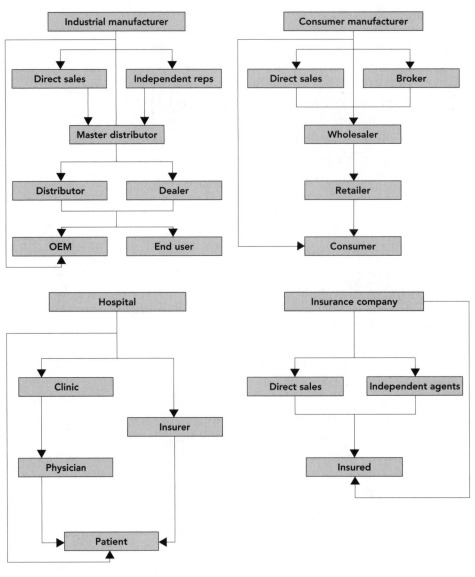

generally buy products, are compensated through discounts off list price, and usually sell to customers out of inventory. The customers could be other resellers, integrators, manufacturers, or the end users. Special types of distributors include value-added resellers (VARs) and dealers.

FIGURE 12.3 *Example Internet Objectives*

- Position a company or brand.

- Generate leads.

- Transact sales.

- Develop customized products.

- Provide technical service.

- Build customer loyalty.

The product manager, as the voice of the customer, should always stay abreast of any changes in where or how target customers (i.e., the end customers for the product) want to buy. This information must be balanced with the ability to maintain a competitive advantage, the brand "fit," and the level of channel conflict.

Where and How Customers Want to Buy

In the Dell example presented earlier, many small businesses (especially those without an internal IT department) like to buy computers from a business that not only supplies the product but also provides the related services. A significant percentage of these customers would not find a direct channel satisfactory. How satisfied are your customers with your existing channel(s)? Ask yourself the following questions:

- Do your target customers like to purchase a bundle of products (perhaps even from competitors) with one invoice? If so, that may suggest a need for an intermediary such as a distributor.
- Do they want 24/7 ordering capabilities?
- Do they want to test the product or see it demonstrated?
- Do they want a product customized to their unique needs?

In answering the question of how customers buy, start with the end user. (The distributors, dealers, wholesalers, and retailers are customers and partners.) How do competitors reach the end customers? Do new channels exist now that weren't available before? If you change the channel, will customers use it? Which customers? Does the channel fit the product?

Ability to Maintain a Competitive Advantage

While developing a go to market strategy that addresses customer preferences, it's also important to determine what can be done to maintain a competitive advantage. If an indirect channel best satisfies customer needs, for example, chances are high that competitors will also be present in the channel. Therefore, your success will depend partly on your ability to motivate channel members to implement the marketing plan for your product.

Sometimes your best chance at maintaining a competitive advantage is through a hybrid channel. Gateway's channel, for example, is between the direct approach used by Dell and the indirect mass retail channels of Hewlett-Packard. The Gateway approach allows customers to create a custom computer, while being able to see tangible products and have a face-to-face discussion with a salesperson. Volvo GM Heavy Truck Corporation also created a hybrid channel. It found that although dealers could predict scheduled maintenance demand quite well, they were not as effective in estimating demand for emergency road-side service. Therefore, Volvo set up a warehouse in Memphis to stock the full line of truck parts and contracted with FedEx to handle the necessary shipments.[5]

In some cases, the advantage comes from selecting the right type of intermediary that provides the appropriate services for the target customer. If you think in terms of "buying distribution services" rather than selling through a distribution channel, your focus will shift to the types of services most appropriate for addressing customer needs. If the customer wants to see the tangible product, a channel with a showroom may be necessary. If customers want to be able to immediately and conveniently buy a product and take it with them, a channel with numerous locations may be required. If the customer wants to have a product delivered and installed, a channel offering those services is critical.

Once the requirements for the channel(s) are established, it is important to determine how to most profitably meet them. Which services can (should) your firm provide, and which ones can (should) intermediaries provide? Even when you determine it is most cost-effective to have the channel (e.g., distributors) provide the services, your firm must monitor the quality of services to avoid damage to brand equity. Remember that cost-effective does not always equate to long-term profitability.

---

5. James Narus and James Anderson, "Rethinking Distribution: Adaptive Channels," *Harvard Business Review,* July-August 1996, p. 114.

Brand Fit

The type of intermediary—or even a specific reseller—may impact your brand equity positively or negatively. Is the technical support adequate? Is the level of customer service sufficient? Is the reseller's brand image consistent with your positioning? When Nike brings out new shoes, it generally sells them through outlets such as Niketown (to maintain a more contemporary fashion image), whereas older styles are sold through the mass discount channels. Huffy discovered the danger of an improper channel fit when it introduced its new Cross Sport bike in the 1990s.

Huffy Corp., the successful $700 million bike maker, did careful research before it launched a new bicycle it dubbed the Cross Sport, a combination of the sturdy mountain bike popular with teenagers and the thin-framed, nimbler racing bike. Huffy conducted two separate series of market focus groups in shopping malls across the country, where randomly selected children and adults viewed the bikes and ranked them. The bikes met with shoppers' approval. So far, so good. In the summer of 1991, Cross Sports were shipped out to mass retailers, such as the Kmart and Toys R Us chains, where Huffy already did most of its business. That was the mistake. As Richard L. Molen, Huffy president and chief executive, explains the company's slipup, the researchers missed one key piece of information. These special, hybrid bikes, aimed at adults and, at $159, priced 15 percent higher than other Huffy bikes, needed individual sales attention by the sort of knowledgeable salespeople who work only in bike specialty shops. Instead, Huffy's Cross Sports were supposed to be sold by the harried general salespeople at mass retailers such as Kmart. Result: "It was a $5 million mistake," says Molen. By 1992, the company had slashed Cross Sport production 7 percent and recorded an earnings drop of 30 percent.[6]

There may be other brand questions a product manager should consider. How will your channel partners be identified? Will you provide them with a graphic mark that indicates their affiliation with your company? Are there specific requirements to earn the right to use this mark? Do your partners benefit from using your brand? Do you benefit from a co-branding relationship? Answering these questions is important since brand development is the product manager's responsibility.

---

6. Christopher Power, "Flops," *Business Week*, August 16, 1993, p. 79.

Reflection Point

What channel changes would improve my ability to get my product to target customers?

- What percent of my target market can be reached with my existing channel structure? What gaps in coverage exist?
- Do I sell to customers the way they want to buy?

- Do existing channels provide a competitive advantage, fit my product's brand, and reduce unnecessary conflict?
- By supplementing the activities of existing channel members, could sales and profitability be improved?

Channel Conflict

Whenever a company has more than one path to the market, there is the potential for channel conflict. Some resellers may resent other channels that offer a lower price point to the same customer. Therefore, companies try to reduce the potential for conflict through various strategies. One approach is to offer different versions of the product to different channels, similar to the Nike example presented earlier. Another approach is to segregate the channels by customer types; for example, one channel may focus on hospitals while another may focus on industrial firms. A third approach, where the conflict may be between direct and independent sales forces, may be to designate certain customers as key accounts to be handled exclusively by the company sales force, or if follow-up work is necessary from the channel, to compensate the channel appropriately.

Ongoing Support

Once the right channel structure is in place, it is still important to support the continued sales efforts. Many companies don't know what their resellers need, or what type of marketing support to provide. The first step for product managers and/or other marketing individuals in the firm is to assess channel partner needs. Should you provide assistance in sales calls on the product? Will additional incentives be necessary? What marketing communications tools are needed?

FIGURE 12.4 *Incentives to Motivate the Channel*

- Discounts
- Sales promotions
- Guarantees
- Spiffs
- Promotional funds

Most B2B product managers, as well as an increasing number of consumer product managers, participate in team selling to resellers in the channel. This requires an understanding of the basic sales process, primarily listening, probing, and "translation" skills. More and more sales practitioners and trainers emphasize the importance of listening to customers a greater percentage of time than talking to them. Listen for needs relevant to your product or service and probe for further clarification. Think about the journalistic approach to gathering information: who, what, when, where, why, and how.

- *Who* are the potential and existing users of this product? Who are the influencers and decision makers?
- *What* problem(s) are they trying to solve? What applications require different usages of the product? What alternatives do they or will they consider?
- *When* did they first identify the need? When does a purchase decision need to be made?
- *Where*, specifically, will the product be used, installed, inventoried? Where did they buy this type of product in the past?
- *Why* are they considering the purchase at this time?
- *How* will the product be used?

Once the sales team has answers to these types of questions, the product manager can help in translating product features and attributes into appropriate benefits and solutions. Some features may be relevant to a particular customer, while others are not. Similarly, some problems may require a creative examination of features and ancillary services.

Beyond the product manager's involvement in team selling, he or she may also be involved in developing marketing support programs for the channel. This could include both incentives (see Figure 12.4) and marketing communications efforts.

Several types of *discounts* may be appropriate for the channel: volume, functional, and long-term contracts. Volume discounts may be appropriate for commodity items requiring intensive distribution. However, they reward distributors on how they buy rather than how they sell. Functional discounts are fees given to channel members performing specific services. Sometimes called "activity-based compensation," functional discounts are appropriate when your product requires specific supporting services (e.g., a showroom, installation services, etc.) to be effective in the market. Long-term discounts attempt to tie a channel member to your firm. They could include a flat price (balancing highs and lows in a turbulent price market such as energy transmission) or a guarantee of no price increases over a given time period.

Sales promotions include activities intended to spur sales in the short term. Contests, for example, may be used to generate excitement for a new product launch. The choice of a prize may be difficult since not all distributors value the same things. Therefore, some companies use "cafeteria incentive programs," allowing the channel members to choose their own prizes. Prizes could include free or partially reimbursed training, additional advertising allowances, and greater cooperative advertising latitude, in addition to trips and cash.

Guarantees made to end customers sometimes make it easier for distributors to sell products. This is particularly true for extended warranties on new products. *Spiffs* (sales promotion incentive funds) are additional compensation given to reseller salespeople for selling your product rather than competitive products. However, care must be taken to avoid causing salespeople to sell to customers where the product fit is questionable, since that may harm long-term brand equity.

Promotional funds generally consist of promotional allowances and cooperative advertising. Promotional allowances refer to rebates or monies given to resellers for their own marketing. Cooperative advertising is a sharing of the cost of advertising when the channel member advertises your product. Both are typically percentages of the sales of your product.

The product manager may also be involved in providing promotional material to sell both *to* and *through* the channel (see Figure 12.5). Material directed to the channel should emphasize the benefits they receive, such as increased throughput, ease of doing business, or greater profitability. For material provided to the channel for them to use with their customers, emphasis should be placed on end customer benefits. This type of "pass-through" literature should be flexible enough for individual distributors and dealers to adapt with their contact information and supply to customers. Sometimes the simplest method is to provide the channel with templates that can be updated quickly. This is relevant even

FIGURE 12.5 *Marketing Support for the Channel*

Provide pass-through materials.
- ad slicks, catalogs, videos, bulletins, CD-ROMs

Design direct marketing campaigns.
- flyers, mail list upgrades

Increase home office promotions.
- Website, press releases, national advertising/PR

Encourage distributor promotions.
- co-op programs, yellow pages, customer seminars, trade shows, open houses

Educate.
- merchandising suggestions, POP displays, advertising basics, communications policies, newsletters

---

if the intermediary is a doctor, contractor, or other referring channel member. Pass-through material might consist of preprinted direct mailers, kits, ad slicks, catalogs, product sheets, videos, bulletins, and CDs. In all cases, product managers should incorporate brand identity guidelines where appropriate.

Product managers might also assist in other ways to improve marketing communications efforts of the channel. They might increase home office promotions to build brand equity and increase customer *pull* through the channel. This is particularly important when channel motivation is low and pulling in new customers can reenergize channel interest. For example, national advertising and public relations, trade show attendance, press releases, and website information can encourage customers to seek out channels for the product or service. For some types of products, educating the channel on advertising basics, merchandising approaches, POP displays, cross-selling opportunities, and communications policies can result in improved performance.

In all communications efforts, consideration should be given to appropriate brand placement. Should your trademark or the reseller's trademark be used in ads, on collateral products, and at trade shows? Too many brand logos can confuse customers and prospects. Therefore, the product manager should evaluate what approach(es) is/are most appropriate for target customers and overall effectiveness.

Reflection Point

What tactical support can I provide to my channels to improve the sales, profitability, and brand equity of my products?

- Have I evaluated channel needs in terms of marketing support for my product?
- What improvements can I make in linking product features and attributes to customer needs and wants?

- What changes can I make in the incentives I provide to channel members to increase their motivation?
- Are my promotional and collateral materials user-friendly and adaptable by the channel?
- Have I created brand procedures as appropriate to unify the customer message through the channel?

KEY POINTS

- Stay abreast of changes in the way your customers want to buy your type of product.
- Creatively explore new go to market approaches.
- Determine whether distribution changes can enhance your competitive edge.
- Maintain control of your brand equity throughout your channels.
- Try to reduce channel conflict by offering different product versions through different channels.
- Provide appropriate incentives to motivate the channel, particularly for new products.
- Provide adaptable communications templates for your resellers to quickly and conveniently apply to their needs.

"GO TO MARKET" CHECKLIST

STRATEGIC FIT

Does your existing channel still help you achieve your
long-term goals?   Yes   No

Have you carefully evaluated where and how your customer
prefers to buy?   Yes   No

Can you maintain a competitive advantage with your current
channels?   Yes   No

Do your current channels enhance your brand equity?   Yes   No

Have you modified your marketing programs to reduce
channel conflict?   Yes   No

TACTICAL SUPPORT

Can you support your channel salespeople effectively on
team sales calls?   Yes   No

Do you provide adequate incentives to motivate the channel?   Yes   No

Do you develop promotional strategies for selling both *to* and
through the channel?   Yes   No

Have you decided on the appropriate balance of push and
pull strategies?   Yes   No

Do you consistently apply appropriate brand logos throughout
the channel?   Yes   No

Index